"Arthur was a better bowle[
unadulterated slogging that br[
back. Spectators, many coming[
ished the ritual of a few orthoc[
before he took aim at the nearest allotments. At headquarters, he terrified the fish in the Tone that winds along the boundary; at Wells, where twice he hit five sixes in an over, the theological students ducked and retreated to the safety of the cathedral pews. Arthur was tall and bronzed, his bowling renowned for its away swing and the distinctive leap before release. There would have been more than two Tests but for the war. He liked a pint, placed an authoritative bet on the horses and seldom lost at cards (his pal Bill Andrews used to say Wellard could memorise every one in the pack). At silly mid-off, he was known to take out his teeth, supposedly to confuse the batsman."

David Frith, writing in *Wisden Cricket Monthly*, acknowledges the aptness of Foot's description of Wellard as a mixture of village blacksmith and England player, but takes a slightly different view of his technique:

"At first something of a rustic hitter, he worked on his batting until he could – reluctantly – defend as well as hit with astonishing power. His driving was scientific, not 'blind', and epitomised the theory that if a ball was smitten hard and high enough, no fieldsman on earth could stop it. His sixes flowed like ack-ack fire – 500 of them – more than anyone else since, in 1910, clearance of the boundary has spelt six runs. No-one has been able to assess exactly how many balls Wellard lost."

Wells is the smallest cathedral city in England and from 1935 to 1951 when Somerset matches were staged at Rowden Road, the ground possessed some of the smallest boundaries in the county game. Having already taken nine wickets in the match against Derbyshire, Wellard came in to bat when Somerset were struggling at 143 for five as they chased 274 to win. He was immediately dropped in the deep off Armstrong and then hit two sixes in the same over which led to the bowler being rested. When Armstrong returned, Wellard didn't score from the first ball of his over but then deposited the next two into the car park before hitting the fourth one straight out of the ground. When it was lost, the replacement ball was dispatched for another two sixes. Wellard ended up with 86 runs, 74 of them being scored with only 15 strokes – seven sixes and eight fours – and Somerset scraped home by one wicket.

Wellard's main rival as the premier master blaster during the 1930s was Jim Smith, the Middlesex and England opening bowler who secured his place in the record books when he scored the game's fastest fifty in May 1938. A typical tailender, he was well aware of his limitations as a batsman. According to Wellard's biographer, Barry Phillips, the Somerset all-rounder was *No Mere Slogger*, but 'Big Jim' Smith, all six foot three inches and 16 stone of him, positively revelled in the fact that he was just that – a serial slogger who hit the ball with an almighty swish of his bat. Essentially, Smith had a single shot in his locker. He would plant one foot either side of the crease and start the stroke with the bat coming down in line with third man before it ended up pointing towards mid-on in the follow-through. It was very simple but very effective and Smith never deviated from this set routine. "If you were fielding near in and he missed the ball," wrote Gerald Brodribb in his book, *Hit for Six*, "you could feel the blast of displaced air."

"I used to slash at virtually every ball," Smith explained not long before he died in 1979. "I can't do to see nine, ten and jack playing about now. Why not have a go, entertain the people? I never had any pretensions about my batting, but sometimes I came off. The catering manager at Lord's used to tell me that the only rest his girls got in the bar was when I batted!"

Middlesex supporters were regularly treated to a feast of

big hitting as Smith smashed sixes all over the place. One went through the windows of the committee room and a few disappeared over the Mound Stand and into St John's Wood Road. He had set out his stall soon after making his county debut in 1934 with a series of quick cameos and in the following year, he equalled the world record by hitting a half-century against Kent in just 14 minutes. Four years later, he claimed the record outright when Middlesex played Gloucestershire at Bristol after warming up by hitting 68 in 20 minutes against Sussex four days earlier. His knock during the innings victory against Gloucestershire should have been over before it began. Going in with Middlesex on 499 for eight, Smith was dropped first ball at long-on by Richard Haynes off Reg Sinfield and never looked back. Two successive fours off Sinfield were followed by a six back over George Emmett's head before he tore into Sinfield's next over. Three consecutive, almost straight, sixes increased the momentum and although Smith's hit-and-miss approach inevitably produced the occasional edge, he reached his half-century with another six off Emmett. It was only his 12th scoring shot and had taken just 11 minutes. His eighth and final six, before he was bowled by a straight one by Emmett, meant he had scored 66 out of 69 runs in 18 minutes. Smith's record, despite the best efforts of Kapil Dev, Ian Botham, Viv Richards, Nathan Astle, Adam Gilchrist and Dimitri Mascarenhas et al, still stands today.

Two months after Smith's historic half-century, Wellard was at it again – causing three balls to be lost during an over against Kent in August 1938 as he hit another five consecutive sixes. This time the victim was Frank Woolley, the England all-rounder who was about to retire from the game after 32 years and hadn't bowled too many of his slow left-arm spinners in the last 10 years. Somerset batted first and made 225 all out with Wellard hitting 57 in 37 minutes as he effortlessly swept the first five balls of Woolley's over for six.

Four of them went out of the ground and with his supply of replacement balls down to just one, the umpire, Alec Skelding, pleaded with Wellard to go easy. Wellard later revealed that he suspected that Woolley had deliberately pitched up the last ball in a gesture to help him complete a full set of sixes but Les Ames, the Kent and England wicket-keeper at the time, when asked about this theory said "doesn't sound like Frank Woolley to me." Whatever Woolley's intentions, Wellard didn't quite get hold of the crucial delivery and Bryan Valentine, fielding near the sightscreen, just managed to get his fingertips to the ball before it landed inside the boundary rope. Wellard took a single and the perfect over – six sixes off six balls – remained as elusive as ever. Woolley withdrew from the attack after conceding 40 runs in his two overs and when Kent batted, he was twice lbw to Wellard – the first time for a duck.

"Have you got something against me Arthur?" he asked as Somerset, with Wellard plundering four more sixes in his second innings and then taking six for 50, won by 27 runs.

For the next 30 years, a pavilion full of prolific batsmen continued to rack up huge totals all over the world, including Majid Khan. He managed to match Wellard's record of five sixes – but not with successive balls – just over a year before Garry Sobers hit the jackpot at St Helen's – ironically against the same opposition and on the same ground. The Pakistan wunderkind had begun his career with Lahore as a pace bowler before switching to occasional off-spin because of a back injury and doubts over the legitimacy of his bouncer. But it was through his graceful and fluent batting that he made his name, playing with a seemingly diffident, almost detached air as he compiled significant and stylish scores in extra quick time.

Having made his debut for Pakistan in Australia in 1964 as an 18-year-old – scoring a duck batting at number eight and taking a couple of wickets – Majid arrived in Britain three years later as a top-order, top-class batsman. He made runs against most of the county sides before failing to reach double figures in either innings in the first Test against England at Lord's. In the tourists' next but one match against Glamorgan in Swansea in August, he hit 37 in a total of 249 for nine declared and after the Welsh side had declared their first innings on 250, Majid launched an amazing assault on off-spinner Roger Davis as he raced to 147 not out in just 89 minutes in Pakistan's second innings.

"Before I started," recalls Majid, "I had made up my mind to go for the fastest hundred of the season. I didn't know anything about any world record for the number of runs or sixes scored off an over – I just went out to hit the ball. I think it was just one of those days when everything went my way. Every time I lashed out, the ball went over the boundary. It wasn't my intention to go after a particular player – Roger or anybody. I was going to go after whoever was bowling and whoever came in the way got belted away."

Majid achieved his target by hitting his hundred in just 61 minutes. Davis, an opening batsman and occasional off-spinner, had been the pick of Glamorgan's bowlers in Pakistan's second innings, taking the first three wickets to fall after opener Faqir Aizazuddin had retired hurt. He finished with three for 98 from 18 overs and remembers making sure that his name would not go down in six-hitting history.

"After Majid hit the first ball of the over for six," recalls Davis, "I thought: 'Hang on – he's going to try to do the six of them.' I sussed it out straightway so I bowled the second one down the leg side. It was extremely wide so there was no way he was going to hit that one for six, Majid missed it and the ball went through to Eifion Jones, our wicket-keeper. I wasn't going to take any chances. As the sixes kept coming, I thought what a good player Majid was. I was trying to bowl properly and they were five fantastic shots."

After the 13th six, it was announced on the public address

system that Majid had broken the world record for scoring the most sixes in an innings. Pakistan's captain, Saeed Ahmed, promptly declared on 324 but the tourists later discovered that Majid was, in fact, three short of making history. The New Zealander, John Reid, had hit 15 sixes for Wellington against Northern Districts in a Plunket Shield game in 1963 when he scored 296.

That superb innings in 1967 led directly to Glamorgan signing Majid as their overseas player for the following season and he found himself fielding at slip when Garry Sobers achieved the maximum off a six-ball over on a late summer Saturday afternoon in Swansea. The West Indian captain had already hit the fastest century of the season for Nottinghamshire against Kent at Dover by taking 77 minutes to reach three figures and he was undoubtedly the star attraction at St Helen's.

That particular August Bank Holiday weekend was an eventful one for British sport. Our athletes were undergoing their last serious test before leaving for the Mexico Olympics by taking on Poland at White City, golfer Peter Townsend won his first major tournament by beating the 19-year-old Bernard Gallacher by three shots, cricket commentator Henry Blofeld was cutting his journalistic teeth by reporting on Arsenal's 2-1 victory over QPR for *The Sunday Express* and Newport County fans at last had something to cheer about. After firing blanks for four games as the new season gathered momentum, their team put four goals past Southend. "Football, to revive the venerable cliché," wrote Ronald Atkin in his round-up for *The Observer,* "is a funny old game."

Indeed it is – just like cricket. As the 40th anniversary of the game's most famous over is celebrated, spare a thought for those Glamorgan supporters who decided to forsake the Nottinghamshire match in the middle of the afternoon and walk to the Vetch Field half a mile away to join a crowd of nearly 9,000 to watch Swansea Town draw 0-0 with

Workington. Those who are still living are still cursing their bad judgment because as they filed out of the Vetch Field at the end of a match which *The Western Mail* described as "a real shocker", Sobers was making hay and history in the sunshine at St Helen's. The papers were right: it was a record that could never be broken: equalled, as it has been three times since, but never beaten because, in cricket, it's just not cricket: you can't get better than six of the best.

A MASTER OF ALL TRADES

When Garry Sobers joined Nottinghamshire in the summer of 1968, it was the cricketing equivalent of Cristiano Ronaldo signing for Derby County at the end of the 2007-08 Premier League season. The world's best player had amazingly decided to throw in his lot with what was, essentially, the worst team in the country. Sobers had agreed to join a side who had finished last in the county championship five times during the previous decade. After propping up the table for two successive seasons, they had rallied slightly to move up to joint 15th in 1967 but to all intents and purposes, Nottinghamshire had hit rock bottom: the only way was up.

The arrival of Sobers at Trent Bridge was the direct result of a momentous sea change in English cricket. With the county game dying on its feet, the MCC belatedly, and very reluctantly, had decided to introduce immediate registration for overseas players in the autumn of 1967. Until then, such cricketers had been forced to live within a county's boundaries for two consecutive years to qualify and many of them, including Sobers, were not prepared to give up their international careers to become eligible. From 1963, overseas players had become a significant feature of the county game through the success of the International Cavaliers. This travelling circus of flamboyant cricketers had unearthed a huge public appetite for one-day matches staged in a simple and spectacular format – similar to the response being generated by Twenty20 as it reinvigorates the modern game today. A team of leading overseas Test stars, current and former England internationals and up-and-coming players from home and abroad would take on most of the counties in a 40-over match on a Sunday. Backed by the Rothmans tobacco firm, the games attracted average crowds of 10,000 and eventually regular television coverage on BBC2. County players relished the freedom created by the opportunity to take on the world's best and the public, around the grounds or in their armchairs, lapped up the entertainment as the big hitters strutted their stuff on the Cavaliers' stage. Although they were superseded by the John Player League in 1969, the International Cavaliers played a key part in persuading the authorities to dispense with the red tape and open up the game from the summer of 1968 to a galaxy of foreign stars – and none of them shone brighter than Garry Sobers.

In 1967's *Wisden*, a year after he had led his team to a 3-1 series win over England, the West Indies captain was the subject of an article by Sir Neville Cardus in which the doyen of writers posed the question: is Sobers the greatest all-round cricketer in history? Cardus then proceeded to analyse the achievements of a first-class career which began when the 16-year-old Sobers took seven wickets for 142 bowling spin in a match for Barbados against the Indians in 1953. Just over a year later, he made his Test debut against England in Kingston – taking four for 75 and making 14 not out and 26 batting at number nine – and from then on, Sobers gradually grew into a devastating batsman and the most complete cricketer to have ever graced the game. As well as his prolific and powerful batting – Cardus summed it up as 'lyrical' – Sobers bowled left-arm fast-medium-pace, orthodox spin and a mixture of chinamen and googlies. And when not batting or bowling, his close fielding was simply breathtaking.

He was only 21 when he spent 10 hours and 14 minutes setting a new world Test record of 365 not out against Pakistan, he did the double of 1,000 runs and 50 wickets in South Australia's Sheffield Shield matches in two of his three seasons Down Under as he helped them win the competition for the first time in 25 years and in the 1966 series against England, he scored 722 runs at an average of 103.14, took 20 wickets at 27.25 and held on to 10 catches.

In concluding his *Wisden* article, "Sobers – The Lion of Cricket", Cardus wrote that "he has betrodden hemispheres of cricket, become a national symbol of his own islands, the representative image on a postage stamp. Best of all, he has generally maintained the *art* of cricket at a time which, day by day – especially in England – threatens to change the game into (a) real industry or (b) a sort of out-of-door "Bingo" cup jousting. He has demonstrated, probably unaware of what he has been doing, the worth of trust in natural-born ability, a lesson wasted on most players here. If he has once or twice lost concentration at the pinch – as he did at Kennington Oval in the fifth Test last year – well, it is human to err, occasionally, even if the gods have lavished on you a share of grace and skill not given to ordinary mortals. The greatest ever? – certainly the greatest all-rounder today, and for decades. And all the more precious is he now, considering the general nakedness of the land."

Over the years, countless less learned but equally fulsome tributes have been paid to the genius of Garry Sobers. The former England captain, Ray Illingworth, spoke for many when he described him as "the greatest all-round player the world has ever seen… he was happy to stand or fall by his belief that cricket, even at Test level, should be entertaining" and one of the most apposite and accurate assessments came from the writer, Lawrence Booth, who summed up Sobers as "a master of all trades and a jack of none." For whoever he played – be it the West Indies, Barbados, South Australia or even Radcliffe in the Central Lancashire League or Norton in the Staffordshire League – Sobers had always delivered and in the summer of 1968, the incredulous cricket-lovers of Nottinghamshire were hoping that he could weave his magic as the new captain of their ailing county side.

There was no doubt that the Trent Bridge committee had pulled off a considerable coup. The editor of *Wisden,* Sydney

Pardon, had devoted a large section of his notes to the signing in the 1968 edition after describing the decision to introduce immediate registration for overseas players as a "bold move" which could save the county championship. The arrival of Sobers at Trent Bridge was hailed as Nottinghamshire's "capture of cricket's greatest prize" following their failure in the 1967 season, for the first time in their history, to win a single championship game. Pardon recalled the impact of the Australian all-rounder, Bruce Dooland, who rescued and then rejuvenated Nottinghamshire in the early 1950s and he later revealed that following MCC's decision, seven counties had made enquiries about signing Sobers. They included Lancashire, Gloucestershire, Northamptonshire and Leicestershire who, having finished joint second with Kent behind champions Yorkshire, must have seemed a more attractive proposition. Although the financial details of Sobers' three-year contract had not been disclosed, Pardon speculated that it "could be worth £7,000 a year, including a flat and a car" – and he wasn't far wrong.

Sobers had become the highest-paid player in the world but, at the age of 31 and with 14 solid years of cricket behind him, he felt the relaxation in the rules had arrived a little too late for him. Had it happened five or six years earlier, then he would have been fitter and in his prime but he still welcomed the chance to play in the English game. The task of sorting out the offers was entrusted to his agent, Bagenal Harvey, who had started his career in sport as business adviser to England's legendary batsman, Denis Compton, and was the brains behind the International Cavaliers.

"Bagenal accepted the offer from Nottinghamshire because it was the best," says Sobers. "A £5,000-a-season salary, accommodation, a car and fares home to Barbados. Trent Bridge suited me nicely. It was one of the best batting pitches in the country – in the days before they used to leave the grass on! – and I had previously made two double centuries there for the West Indies. The team had been near the bottom in previous seasons and had no Test players or players on the fringe of the England side. They were mostly good professionals, no stars but a lot of hard workers and enthusiasts."

One such enthusiast was Graham Frost, a local lad who had been training to become a buyer in the building industry before deciding to go full-time with Nottinghamshire in that particular season. The 21-year-old middle-order batsman had made his first-class debut as a semi-professional against the touring Indians at Trent Bridge in 1967. Like most of the county's playing staff, old and new, he had to pinch himself when the identity of the new captain was revealed.

"I can always remember when Garry arrived for preseason training at Trent Bridge," says Frost. "He never used to train because he was always playing all the year round but he took part in a practice match on the square and guess who went in to face him bowling his quicker stuff? I actually played him quite well and caressed him through the covers with a couple of off drives – I felt 10 foot tall! Facing the great Garry Sobers was one of the best moments of my life – it's something I'll never forget."

Having joined Nottinghamshire in 1966 after spending eight years with Middlesex, Bob White was one of the "hard workers" Sobers found himself playing alongside. An opening or middle-order batsman, he only became a regular at Lord's after making 1,355 runs at 33.57 in 1963 – the only season he passed four figures. When his form fell away, White moved to Trent Bridge where he developed into a good all-rounder who bowled tidy off-spin – especially after Sobers arrived.

"I was in South Africa when I heard about Garry signing for Nottinghamshire," he recalls. "I couldn't believe it! He was coming to play for us? The year before we hadn't won a single match in the championship and our only win was against Durham in the first round of the Gillette Cup. Before Garry came, we had a decent side but we were playing on such a good pitch at Trent Bridge that we just couldn't get a result. He changed all that – he got results all over the place.

"It was an eye-opener playing in the same team as him. He opened doors for us and it was only when you were batting from the other end that you knew how good he was. We were both left-handers and when we were facing Fred Trueman, who was admittedly past his best, I was fending off the balls from my ribs and Garry was whipping them away for four. I just wondered how the bloody hell he did it!

"He gave me a lot of opportunities as a bowler. I was the club's off-spinner and that was good enough for Garry. He didn't question how good or bad you were and I never heard him criticize anybody. He gave you the ball and it was up to you to show him how good you were.

"Off the field, Garry, like me, was interested in horses and that was the one big reason why we were friends. We had common interests – cricket and horses. I was a fellow punter but I'm not a professional gambler or a candidate for Gamblers Anonymous. I go to Nottingham races but just for enjoyment. I'm interested in what happens. I might have a bet, I might not."

White had met Sobers in passing two years earlier during the West Indies tour of England. In his second game, the captain took apart Nottinghamshire's attack with a devastating display of batting at Trent Bridge. After an uncertain start, he ended up hitting 153 out of a total of 221 in 160 minutes with 20 fours and five sixes.

"Everything that could be said has already been said about the incredible Sobers," wrote Neville Foulger in *The Nottingham Guardian Journal*. "The only thing I can add is that Sobers merely doubled his reputation yesterday."

"During his innings," White recalls, "Garry became a bit bored and you could see that he made his mind up to hit our left-arm medium-pace bowler, Carlton Forbes, to every point of the compass. He started off late-cutting him to third man and he went round the clock – extra cover, mid-off, mid-on and over mid-wicket to square leg. He was so much in control that he picked out the shots one by one and at the end of one particularly harsh over, he had the biggest grin you'd ever seen on his face. Carlton ended up with one for 86 off 23 overs, I had one for 77 off 12 but I eventually caught Garry in front of the pavilion off Keith Gillhouley, a slow left-arm orthodox bowler."

"If there had been any low clouds, the ball would surely have disappeared into them," wrote Foulger, "and the wait for it to come down must have been an agony of time and control for White. But, to almost a football-style roar, he was ready and waiting to make a very difficult catch look very simple."

"As this bloody great skier came down," says White, "I remember hearing all the West Indian team in the pavilion shouting "back the ball! back the ball!" In other words, they were backing the ball rather than me because they didn't think I would catch it. It was up there for what seemed like weeks but I managed to hang on to it. Garry had to walk past me on his way back to the pavilion and he smiled as he went past to suggest 'well done!' – I think he'd had enough by then!"

White was one of a number of Nottinghamshire players whose careers flourished under Sobers. Brian Bolus was another. In 1963, he had decided to move south from Yorkshire when his native county backed the younger and relatively unknown Geoffrey Boycott to open their innings. He settled down well at Trent Bridge and made his England debut against the West Indies at Headingley in 1963 when he hit the first ball he faced from Wes Hall for four. He never let his country down, averaged a very respectable 41.33 in his 12 Test innings and was unlucky to be replaced in the England team by Boycott who formed an impressive opening pairing with Surrey's John Edrich.

"I won seven caps and then no more – quite rightly," admits Bolus. "In 1964, the selectors gave me ample opportunity to retain my place but I didn't play well enough. I then became consumed with theory and got into this habit of playing too much with my pads which was self-destructive. After 1963, I was on a gradual decline for four seasons and then Garry Sobers arrived on the scene and my form really picked up. Whatever other people may say after looking at the averages, Garry was in a class of his own. When he arrived, there was a complete reversal in our fortunes, the spirit of the side was such that people were playing and feeling better and Garry was the man who galvanized us – he was an inspiration to us all. We didn't go on to the field feeling that the best job we could do was to draw – we went on thinking we could win. It was never a case of him coming into the dressing room and telling us what to do. He just went out and played – he led by example not by tactics.

"We had the greatest player on God's earth playing for us but Garry wasn't as good at being captain as he was at playing the game. He was fearless and he led from the front. He would occasionally give you advice but he allowed you to do your job – he had faith in the other players. His style of captaincy was too optimistic for the talent he had underneath him. Garry could get wickets when the wicket was flat but the rest of us weren't too good at that. There were times when he made the mistake of thinking we were all as good as he was – and we weren't. He sometimes made over-generous declarations but his attitude wasn't cavalier. He just thought we had a chance of winning and if things went our way, it would be OK but our talents didn't match up to his. There were other occasions when his spirit of adventure brought results – like the win in the six sixes game against Glamorgan at Swansea."

Mike Smedley was another of the "hard workers" in the Nottinghamshire team when Sobers arrived at Trent Bridge.

The 26-year-old Yorkshireman was a middle-order right-handed batsman who had made his debut in 1964 and won his county cap two years later. In 1967, he had finished second to Bolus in the county's averages having hit nearly 1,500 runs in the championship with a top score of 124.

"We had people on the Notts committee at the time who wanted the best and they went out and got the best," says Smedley. "It was fantastic playing with the world's greatest cricketer on a daily basis. We had come across Garry in tour matches but to see him and play with him every day was just awesome. I batted with him in a lot of games and it took a little while to adjust but, having done that, it made things a lot easier. It took the pressure off having Garry at the other end keeping the score moving along. Occasionally he'd say things like 'I think you could hit this chap over mid-wicket' and 'we need to get a move on' if we were chasing and he thought the run rate was going up. It was difficult to appreciate what a great player he was until you played with him. We would be set a target by opposing captains with Garry in mind and that meant that some of the other players had to bat a little bit better as well – which we did."

The West Indian wicket-keeper, Deryck Murray, had been able to turn out for Nottinghamshire since 1966 as an overseas player because he was studying at Cambridge University and therefore qualified under residency rules. Having made his Test debut in 1963 and become a good friend of Sobers, Murray was instrumental in the West Indies captain coming to Trent Bridge.

"We were very poor – to put it mildly," he recalls. "We were almost resigned to finishing bottom of the championship but everyone around Garry just wanted to lift their game so they were able to say they deserved to be on the same field as him."

"I used to come on first change and Garry's record shows that he always got into the opposition's top order," recalls

Mike Taylor, a right-arm medium-pace bowler who had made his Nottinghamshire debut four years earlier. "It's much easier if you're bowling to new batsmen, or those down the order, than if you come on when the opposition are 140 for none and smashing you all around the park. Garry got Notts into good positions – I was bowling at new batsmen with fielders around the bat and it was a great position for me to be in."

From the outset, Sobers rarely failed to make his mark with either bat or ball. In his very first match for his new employers, he took three for 28 off 11.2 overs and hit a match-winning 75 not out as Nottinghamshire beat Lancashire by three wickets at Trent Bridge in the first round of the Gillette Cup in April. He began his championship career by taking five for 25 and making 59 not out in a total of 104 in a rain-affected match against Middlesex at Trent Bridge in early May and after another three draws, Nottinghamshire looked to be heading for their first win of the season when they played Warwickshire at home in early June. Much was made of the eagerly anticipated head-to-head confrontation between four of the West Indian superstars – all-rounder Sobers, batsman Rohan Kanhai, wicket-keeper Deryck Murray and spinner Lance Gibbs. In fact, the game was billed as Nottinghamshire's Sobers and Murray versus Warwickshire's Kanhai and Gibbs and was later described in *Wisden* as an "astonishing" match. Neither Sobers nor Murray had much to do with the visitors being skittled out for just 93 – medium-pacers Mike Taylor (six for 42) and David Halfyard (three for 20) doing the damage – but they helped Nottinghamshire reach 282 with the skipper scoring 54 and his wicket-keeper friend falling just eight runs short of a century. Warwickshire, chasing 189, were then reduced to six for three when Kanhai and Billy Ibadulla came together.

"They were beaten, packing their bags," recalls Bob White. "I remember there was a bit of professional jealously between Sobers and Kanhai – they were West Indian rivals rather than team-mates – and when Kanhai came in, Garry set him up for the hook shot. It was the first time I'd seen it happen. He waited until Kanhai was at the crease and dropped a fielder back at deep square as if to say 'I'm going to knock your bloody head off!' But Garry was too clever for Kanhai. He didn't bowl a bouncer but a short one, Kanhai got in position to hook it and the ball hit the splice of the bat and dollied to gully where my wife could have caught it. I won't tell you who it was but he dropped it and Kanhai went on to make 253. The next over, Billy Ibadulla, who hadn't faced a ball, was put down at first slip off Carlton Forbes and he made 147 not out. They put on 402 for the fourth wicket in six and three-quarter hours and the game ended in a draw. I only saw Garry lose his temper on the field twice – and that Kanhai dropped catch was the first time. He was absolutely livid but he didn't say anything – he didn't need to."

But Nottinghamshire didn't have to wait long to break their championship duck. A week later they travelled down to Taunton and although Sobers failed twice with the bat, his seven wickets in the match, including five for 31 in Somerset's first innings, helped secure a three-wicket victory to kick-start their season. In the next game at Lord's, the skipper scored his first Nottinghamshire century but it wasn't enough to prevent Middlesex inflicting a first defeat of the season on his new club. Graham Frost has fond personal memories of that rain-affected match.

"I batted twice in a day on a bomb site of a pitch," he recalls. "Middlesex made 305 on the first day and then I top scored with 37 out of 115 in our first innings. I went in at number eight and carried my bat and because Brian Bolus had broken his thumb, I was promoted up the order when we were asked to follow on. 'Keep your pads on' Garry said when I arrived back in the pavilion, 'You're opening!'

"Ian Moore and I made a good start and then after a couple of wickets had fallen, Garry came in and we put on

86 – with me getting 39 and Garry going on to make 100. In the end, we reached 252 and Middlesex easily knocked off the runs but it was great playing at Lord's and seeing Garry hit a century."

Four days later, another captain's innings of 95 not out and four wickets for just 15 runs in 11 overs helped Nottinghamshire brush aside Worcestershire to reach the last eight of the Gillette Cup. It was during the quarter-final tie against Gloucestershire at Trent Bridge in early July that Bob White witnessed Sobers losing his temper for the second time when he produced a refreshing example of his trademark brand of sportsmanship. To Sobers, cricket was a game to be enjoyed. You played hard but you played fair and, above all, honestly. From the time he first picked up a bat, Sobers always walked if he knew he had hit a ball and he took a dim view of anyone who tried to bend the rules. Gloucestershire won the toss and scored 296 for eight from their 60 allotted overs. Nottinghamshire made a steady start and Sobers arrived at the crease when his side were 78 for three. He put on 114 for the fourth wicket with Mike Smedley and then when Deryck Murray was out without scoring, Sobers was joined at the wicket by White.

"Garry was absolutely murdering Mike Procter and company," recalls White. "I was just holding an end up and after we'd put on 24 for the fifth wicket, I got an inside edge on a ball which lodged in the top of my pad. Garry called for a run but I didn't go because I knew it should have been a dead ball. I started to bend my knee to scoop it out but before I knew where I was, their wicket-keeper, Barrie Meyer, hit me from behind, knocked me flat on my face, picked up the ball, threw it to Tony Windows at the other end and he ran me out. The umpires let them get away with it and Garry was livid. Almost straightaway, he played a shot in anger to a ball from Tony, it went straight up in the air and the skier was caught by Procter. As Garry walked off, he told their captain,

Arthur Milton: 'If you want to win like that, you can do'. David Halfyard and Mike Taylor nearly won the match for us but, in the end, we lost by 25 runs. Garry was very annoyed because he felt that I'd been cheated out."

But speaking from his home in South Africa, Meyer, who became a Test umpire after spending 15 years with Gloucestershire, insists that White's dismissal was perfectly legitimate. From what he can remember, Sobers and White were going for a run.

"I didn't think it was a dead ball – it was active because they were running," he recalls. "If Bob had just left the ball in his pad, stood his ground or got back into his crease and not attempted a run, then there would have been no problem. As far as I remember, the ball actually came out of Bob's pad and dropped on the wicket. I went to pick it up and I must have bumped into him but it wasn't a deliberate charge as he has claimed. If he was going for the run, I felt I had the right to go for the ball. I would have been a fool not throw it to the other end – I had no option. If the umpires had seen something wrong with it, they would have called a dead ball afterwards and said something to me or Arthur but they were quite happy."

"It was helter skelter and Notts were going quite well," recalls Gloucestershire's Tony Brown. "Garry was probably feeling a bit miffed, he had a thrash at the ball and suffered the consequences. It was unfortunate that he and Arthur exchanged words. It was a very strange situation because here you had two of the most gentlemanly and sportsmanlike cricketers you could ever wish to find anywhere. I know that Arthur was very upset about what happened in that particular incident but the best way Garry could have dealt with it would have been to knock off the runs."

Nottinghamshire were drawing too many matches to mount a concerted challenge for the county championship but Sobers inspired a 56-run win over Lancashire at

Southport by taking three for 38 and then hitting 77 not out before another five-wicket haul and a crucial unbeaten 57 led to victory over Derbyshire by six wickets. In another draw at Northampton in early August, he passed 1,000 runs and reached 50 wickets for the season and in their next game against the eventual runners-up, Kent, at Dover, Sobers showed just why Nottinghamshire had broken the bank to sign him. Bowling fast-medium, he finished with seven for 67 as Kent scored 235 and then made only 17, batting at number seven, in a total of 228. As Kent threatened to recover from a poor start which left them at 64 for four in their second innings, Sobers brought himself on and, bowling his spinners, picked up another four wickets. Nottinghamshire needed 186 in just over two hours, so the captain led from virtually the front by coming in at number three with the score at 38 for one and single-handedly winning the match. He scored 51 out of a total of 71 in his first 40 minutes and his second fifty came even faster as he recorded the quickest century of the season in just 77 minutes. It was a majestic performance containing two sixes and 18 fours as Sobers hit an unbeaten 105 and Nottinghamshire won by seven wickets with five overs to spare. As 1969's *Wisden* noted, "not even the most ardent Kent supporter would deny that this was Sobers' match ... Kent were left with the final "Sobering" thought of what might happen next time they meet the West Indies captain. Last time – at Canterbury, in 1966, when playing for his country, he took nine for 49 – the best bowling performance of his career."

Four draws, a win and a defeat in their next six games meant Nottinghamshire needed to beat Glamorgan in their last match of the season for Sobers to win a wager he had made with Bunty Ames, the wife of former Kent and England wicket-keeper, Les Ames, the previous March. Ames was managing the MCC party when England beat the West Indies 1-0 in a five-match series.

"After a day's play at the Kensington Oval in the third Test," recalls Sobers, "I was sitting down at a cocktail party when Bunty asked me what sort of position I could get Notts to in the county championship.

"'I'll get them to the top four,' I said. It was a rash statement to make because I hadn't met their players and knew little about their strengths and weaknesses – I hadn't a clue.

"'They're not that good,' she said. 'Do you want to bet on it?'

"I wasn't a man to spurn a bet and she promised she would give me six bottles of champagne if I managed to lift Notts into the top six by the end of the season."

The Nottinghamshire players travelled across to Swansea from Portsmouth on Friday 30th August immediately after their drawn match with Hampshire had, unusually, failed to produce a meaningful contribution from their captain. Sobers took no wickets in either Hampshire innings and scored 22 and 12 as Notts ended up chasing more than 200 to win on the final day. By this stage of the season, Graham Frost had firmly established himself as number three in the batting order but he still had certain more menial duties to perform.

"In those days," he recalls, "the kit wagon, a Dormobile, was the responsibility of the new boy – you had to drive it to earn your stripes. Four players took their cars from Nottingham to Portsmouth and then on to Swansea but I drove the kit wagon by myself and joined everyone else at The Dolphin Hotel."

Frost was grateful to have been given the opportunity by Sobers to bat higher up the order so early in his career although, in truth, his promotion had been far from a resounding success. Before the Glamorgan game, he averaged only 16.51 in his 39 innings and had scored only 17 and 14 against Hampshire. Frost had played in all but three of the 27 championship games and wanted to end his first season as a regular on a high note and repay the faith shown in him by his captain. But he had little inkling that his next innings – his third half-century of the summer – would prove crucial in the subsequent creation of a world record.

When Frost and his Nottinghamshire team-mates arrived at St Helen's on the Saturday morning, the sun was shining, an expectant Bank Holiday crowd was starting to gather at the ground and everything was set fair for whoever won the toss. Glamorgan's chances of lifting the championship had disappeared with Yorkshire's 60-run victory over Surrey and their own 100-run defeat by Derbyshire the previous day but, having finished 14th in 1967, a win in their penultimate game would underline their surprising renaissance. Nottinghamshire – and especially Sobers who was keen to collect his champagne – were looking for a seventh victory in their final match to confirm their impressive improvement under the leadership of their imperious captain. Glamorgan's Tony Lewis tossed the coin, Sobers called correctly and then decided to bat on what appeared to be a very inviting wicket. It turned out to be a terrific track but few, if any, of the players, officials or supporters who were present at St Helen's on that historic day could have imagined that 36 of the 471 runs scored would be acquired in such a short space of time and in such a sensational way.

THE CALM BEFORE THE STORM

J ust before half past eleven, Bob White and Brian Bolus
emerged from the away dressing room at St Helen's and
made their way tentatively down the long, concrete stairway leading to the playing area of the ground.
Nottinghamshire's opening batsmen couldn't wait to get to
the bottom – not just because the 67 steps made it a rather
hazardous journey in their full kit but because, as two experienced professionals, they knew a good wicket when they
saw one. They wanted to make the most of Garry Sobers'
good fortune in winning the toss. As they strode to the
middle – a strip on the Gorse Lane side far away from the
adjacent rugby pitch – Bolus, in particular, with an average of
nearly 33, was rubbing his gloves with glee at the prospect of
rounding off the season with a big score.

"In those days," he recalls, "the Swansea wicket looked
like plasticine – there was so much clay in it – and you either
got lots of runs or you were bowled out for not many. The
pitch was beautiful – as flat as a pancake."

The two men were not to be disappointed. White walked
to the Mumbles Road End, took guard, had a last look at the
field and settled down to receive the opening ball of the
innings from Ossie Wheatley. After not scoring from the first
five deliveries, White cracked the last one away for four
before Bolus took two runs off Malcolm Nash's first over
from the Mumbles Road End to ease himself off the mark.

"It was a lovely fine day, there was a good crowd, a good
pitch and a small boundary," recalls White. "There was no
doubt about what we were going to do when Garry won the
toss."

Wheatley, and particularly Nash, who was bowling his
usual left-arm fast-medium seamers, initially managed to

keep it tight. Then Wheatley was hit for a couple of fours by White in his third over before being taken off two overs later while Nash was replaced after conceding nine runs in his sixth over. After a quick burst from fast bowler Tony Cordle from the Pavilion End, skipper Tony Lewis turned to the reliable off-spinner, Don Shepherd, while Peter Walker, Glamorgan's orthodox left-arm spinner, wheeled away from the Mumbles Road End in a 20-over spell.

"Swansea was never a very good place for medium-pace or swing and seam bowlers," recalls Walker. "It was essentially a spinner's pitch. The ball didn't bounce very high, you had to bowl a lot of overs to get the wickets but on the other hand it did turn a bit – that's why I ended up bowling 32 overs in that innings."

Although the runs flowed less freely, the score moved on apace with White the dominant partner and Bolus seemingly content to keep things ticking over with a series of singles and the occasional four and six. White reached 50 in 60 minutes, the hundred partnership arrived after 90 minutes and with no sign of a breakthrough, Lewis replaced Shepherd with Brian Lewis, a 23-year-old off-spinner who had started to feature regularly in the Glamorgan side during the season. He opened with a maiden, conceded a single in his next over and then had White caught at mid-off by Wheatley in his third over for 73.

"Ossie was about six foot four" recalls White, "and he was probably the only person on the bloody ground – apart from their other six-footer, Peter Walker – who would have caught it! Brian and I put on 126 for the opening partnership. I must have been playing pretty well because I outscored him. He was reputed to be a quick scorer and I was supposed to be a blocker so I must have been in good nick."

White's dismissal 10 minutes before lunch put Graham Frost out of his misery. While he was obviously pleased that Nottinghamshire had made such a good start, the first wicket down found waiting around to bat a nerve-racking business and as he made his way out to the middle, Frost was hoping that he wouldn't be forced into making the return journey any time soon.

"The longer you wait, the more anxious you get," he says, "and I remember that the match was played on a wicket right on the far side of the square away from the rugby pitch so it was the longest walk for a first-baller in the land – if not the world. There are that many steps down from the pavilion and then you have to go across to the square to the wicket. But Brian and Bob had been doing well and I fancied myself to make some runs."

After a sticky start in which Frost survived a couple of chances – newspaper reports described him as "fortunate" and "lucky" – he settled down to play perhaps the most significant innings of his short career. He and Bolus took the score to 160 for one by lunch and in the afternoon session, Frost was able to loosen the shackles and really attack the bowling.

"After an opening partnership like ours," he recalls, "it was very important to try and keep the score running. My aim was basically to give Brian the strike which I did quite successfully – except that it really restricted me a little as I tried to force the pace. The wicket was quite slow and Brian Lewis and Peter Walker weren't the easiest of bowlers to get away. Peter was a very tall man who bowled left-arm spin to his fields very well. Going in at number three, I was quite used to facing the new ball when runs were a bit easier to come by but after our big opening stand, the field was set to contain and I found it a bit difficult to pierce the infield."

But inspired by Bolus, who was particularly strong off his legs and picked up plenty of runs through the short boundary at the town end, Frost gradually grew in confidence. As the correspondent in *The Observer* commented, "Bolus continued on his merry way and Frost joined in the fun." Having already hit Walker for six, Bolus did the same to Lewis and Frost started to make his presence felt. He helped Nottinghamshire pick up their first batting point by dispatching Lewis for nine runs in the 61st over before another six runs off a Walker over saw the all-rounder being replaced at the Pavilion End by Nash. As the opening bowler marked out his run-up, some spectators noticed that it wasn't as long as usual – and that Nash was about to bowl around, rather than over, the wicket to Frost. What was going on? It would soon all become clear.

Earlier in the week, the Kent left-arm spinner, Derek 'Deadly' Underwood, had taken nine wickets as England beat Australia by 226 runs in the fifth Test at The Oval. On a rain-affected pitch, he snapped up four wickets in 27 balls with just six minutes left of play to ensure that England squared the series. Underwood's career-best return of seven for 50 in Australia's second innings meant he also reached 100 wickets for the season. It was also a performance which had given huge encouragement to Nash as he prepared for Glamorgan's penultimate game of the summer. With Nottinghamshire apparently heading for a declaration, Tony Lewis finally decided to grant Nash his wish: he could bowl his orthodox left-arm spin rather than his normal seam-up.

"Malcolm had been pleading with me for months to let him try out his spinners," recalls Lewis, "because Underwood was the star of the day with his left-arm medium or slow left-arm orthodox bowling which was proving extremely successful. Malcolm felt he could bowl as well as, if not better, than Underwood. That was Malcolm's style and his confidence served him well because he got more than 900 wickets in his career. I remember Notts were going to declare at some stage, it seemed like a good time to give Malcolm a go and the rest is history. On this fateful day, it was Nash the Underwood lookalike who bowled around rather than over the wicket. If he wanted to try his Underwood stuff, it was in our interest to bowl him during a day's cricket which was steering towards a declaration. I thought he should be bowling right at the end of the innings because it would turn a bit and we could find out more about his spinners."

"Tony asked me to bowl a couple of overs of my 'other stuff' to see if we could buy a wicket," says Nash, now living in California. "Tony's comments about Derek Underwood are reasonably correct because we had discussed the possibility of me doing an Underwood-type thing for Glamorgan as well. There could maybe have been a transition from my new-ball bowling to something similar to what Underwood was purveying on the county scene and for England. My orthodox slow left-arm was considerably slower than Underwood's – he was much quicker than orthodox. In the game against Nottinghamshire, it was a joint decision between me and Tony to let me have a go at using my slower stuff to try to get a wicket."

"People should remember that Malcolm was a wonderful opening bowler in his own right," says Walker, "but he always wanted to try out his spinners and he reckoned he could bowl slow left-arm as well as anybody in the country. That was typical of Malcolm – he had no doubts at all about his own ability."

The experiment paid off almost immediately when Nash broke up another impressive stand between two batsmen who were starting to run riot. At the Mumbles Road End, not even the normally miserly Shepherd could halt the avalanche of runs as Bolus smashed him for three sixes in successive overs. The hundred partnership came up after 71 minutes and Frost brought up his half-century with 11 runs off one over from the recalled Cordle – including his only six and his fifth four. But after conceding a single in his first two overs, Nash then removed Frost.

"I was out trying to hit Malcolm over the top and was caught by Tony Lewis at mid-off," recalls Frost. "That was one of the most important fifties of my career because I played a key part in providing the platform for Garry to hit his six sixes. I always tried to bat positively and I think sometimes it was my downfall. I got out that day playing not for myself but for the side. I think I earned my corn in that game."

Frost and Bolus had certainly maintained the momentum of the Nottinghamshire innings by putting on 132 in 86 minutes and, having been joined by Mike Smedley with the score at 258 for two, Bolus, in particular, continued to push the score along. Smedley appeared to be in good nick – having scored 65 and 13 against Hampshire a few days earlier to reach 1,000 runs for the season but he made a scratchy start.

"When I came in," recalls Smedley, "Malcolm was bowling his slower variety which was a little bit harder to get away straightaway. He bowled seam-up very well, he used to swing the ball in a bit and although lacking a little pace, it was always accurate. He bowled his spinners not quite so well – he didn't have quite as much control with them."

Walker returned for a third spell – his second from the Mumbles Road End – and Bolus hit him for another six before finally holing out at mid-off from the bowling of Nash just before four o'clock. The fielder was Alan Rees, the former Welsh rugby outside-half who had replaced the former Welsh international footballer, Trevor Ford, who, in turn, had been a substitute fielder for Wheatley at the start of the afternoon session. During the lunch interval, Wheatley had complained of sore shins and 45-year-old Ford, who was down in South Wales on holiday, volunteered to take his place.

"Give me some kit and I'll play," he told skipper Lewis. The offer was readily accepted and Ford fielded at mid-off for half an hour without touching the ball before Rees arrived from his home at nearby Port Talbot to relieve him as the official twelfth man.

"Although I got 140 that day, the best knock of our innings, apart from Garry's, was by Bob White," says Bolus.

"A lot of people don't know that, like Garry, I hit six sixes too – but it took me nearly four hours!"

With the score at 289 for three, the West Indian wicket-keeper, Deryck Murray, strolled to the wicket. His unbeaten 35 against Hampshire meant he was just 52 short of 1,000 runs for the season but three balls later, Murray was trudging back to the pavilion after being bowled by Nash for a duck.

"That was a terrible ball," recalls Nash. "It was a china-man out of the back of my hand and it almost bounced twice as it went under the bottom of his bat."

"I don't remember my dismissal with a great deal of pleasure," says Murray. "It was a long hop and my shot is not one of the ones in my career that I'm proud of. I was very embarrassed by it."

If not in trouble, Nottinghamshire were starting to wobble and the stage was set for the arrival of their captain who was expected to bat at number six. But Sobers, who according to Trevor Bailey in his 1976 biography of the West Indian skipper, had "a passion for gambling", had only just returned from visiting a local bookmakers. So in place of the world's greatest all-rounder out came John Parkin, a local player who had been called into the team as a late replace-ment. By his own admission, the unassuming middle-to-late-order batsman never quite made it at county level. Having joined Nottinghamshire as a 20-year-old in 1965, he was not so much a bits-and-pieces player as a bit-part player. Unbeknown to him, Parkin was about to be handed an his-toric walk-on role against Glamorgan.

"I was at home in Kimberley, near Nottingham when the message came through to go down to Swansea," he recalls. "I rang up Trent Bridge and spoke to Roger Vowles, the assis-tant secretary, who told me that with Ian Moore and Carlton Forbes both out injured, Richard Bielby, our twelfth man against Hampshire, and I would come into the side. I drove down to Swansea on the Friday afternoon and evening and met up with the other players who had come across from Portsmouth. To be honest, I think I was just making up the numbers in the last game of the season."

In retrospect, it's difficult to disagree with Parkin's assessment. He had played in only eight championship games during the summer and his 11 innings had garnered only 89 runs with a top score of 20 not out. He hadn't appeared in the first team for five weeks – making six and seven batting at number eight in an 87-run defeat by Hampshire at Worksop at the end of July. He normally went in after Sobers who was reluctant to bat higher up the order.

"Garry always went in at number six," says White, "and it was a bone of contention with us when the 40-over game started. It was ridiculous that the jokers had used up 36 overs and the greatest cricketer in the world was going in with four overs left! We had a hell of a job getting him to bat number three. He said he'd been brought up by the West Indies captain, Frank Worrell, to bat number six where he could assess the match. I'd say to him that he should go in first but he wouldn't hear of it. He played according to the state of the game – which is why he liked batting at number six. The whole point in the Glamorgan game was that it was such a good pitch that he didn't expect us to get out. He wasn't being derelict in his duty – he never put gambling before cricket. He probably thought he had some time to spare – if Bob White could get a 70 at almost a run a ball then it must be a bloody good pitch and he wouldn't be needed for a while. Garry was in his blue gabardine suit rather than his kit when he was due to go in. As John went out to the wicket, I remember Garry looking out of the dressing room window.

"'I'd better get changed," he said. 'I think we need a few quick runs.'

"That was the frame of mind Garry was in when he went out to bat and I wonder if he'd gone in when he should have gone in, would he have scored the six sixes? The situation in the match would have been different and although you can't predict what would have happened, it's a good bet that he wouldn't have hit the six sixes."

Parkin will never forget the moment he came out of the St Helen's dressing room and walked to the top of the concrete stairway. The Bank Holiday crowd were buzzing with anticipation. Glamorgan were fighting back and Nottinghamshire appeared becalmed. Two wickets had fallen in quick succession, the run rate had dropped dramatically and the man who every supporter in the ground had come to see, the star attraction, the top of the bill, was about to make his entrance.

"I was only on the Nottinghamshire staff for four years," says Parkin, "and while I was a pro, I felt that I was never quite up to the mark. I was always looking up to the other players and I just felt I was on the one level below them. That feeling came back to me when I stood at the top of the steps at St Helen's and everybody looked at me and realised it wasn't Garry – I could almost hear the sigh of disappointment."

With Murray having been bowled by the last ball of Nash's 13th over, Parkin had a few moments to prepare for what would turn out to be the most memorable innings of his career. Smedley, having scored just 13 in his 25 minutes at the crease, suddenly burst into life and hit six runs off Walker before Parkin opened his account by scoring three from the next over from Nash and then picking up another two off Walker. Smedley then took a liking to Nash's experimental spinners by hitting him for two fours in an over but Parkin struggled to make any headway against Walker who bowled his fourth and last maiden of the day.

"I can't remember much about the 15 minutes I batted with Mike," says Parkin. "I just played every ball as it came and tried to score runs as quickly as possible – as Garry had said he wanted us to do."

After the pair had put on 19, the moment that everyone had been waiting for finally arrived when the fifth wicket fell.

With the Nottinghamshire total standing at 308, Smedley was out — caught again at mid-off by Tony Lewis to give Nash a very commendable return of 16-3-42-4.

"The experiment had worked pretty well," recalls Nash, "so why change? I felt we were getting wickets and I was just doing what needed to be done."

It was time for Garry Sobers to enter the arena and as Smedley headed off back across the pitch to begin climbing the 67 steps, a murmur of expectation swept around St Helen's as the skipper made his way to the middle. Just walking to the wicket, Sobers was a sight to behold as Henry Blofeld explained in his book, *Cricket's Great Entertainers*:

"He was an incomparable athlete and the first thing one noticed about Sobers, which gave off a wealth of advanced publicity about all that was to come, was his walk. From the moment he appeared on the pavilion steps with that light, angular, lissom walk, one knew that one was in the presence of a remarkable sportsman. He glided to the wicket and this approach heightened the anticipation of what was to follow. Some batsmen shuffle, some walk like mechanical men, some stride and some just appear in the middle without giving anyone the faintest idea of how they got there, and often bat in the same way, but Sobers' approach made everyone sit up."

If, by chance, it didn't on that August Bank Holiday Saturday in Swansea, then Sobers' actions soon did. "Somehow one sensed that something extraordinary was going to happen when Sobers sauntered to the wicket," recorded *Wisden*. "With over 300 runs on the board for the loss of only five wickets, he had the right sort of platform from which to launch a spectacular assault, and the manner in which he immediately settled down to score at a fast rate was ominous."

After the success of his new style of bowling, Nash was delighted when no runs were scored from his first three balls to the Nottinghamshire captain. But, in a foretaste of what was to come, Sobers then smacked the next two balls to the boundary as he set in motion what would turn out to be a truly remarkable captain's innings.

"I went out there with the idea of getting some quick runs because we wanted to declare," says Sobers. "Glamorgan could have got to second or third in the championship and we were poised to finish fourth if we beat them. So the scene was set with everything to play for – not to mention my bottles of champagne – and I thought I would try to make a game of it. When I went out to bat, there were quite a few runs on the board – Brian Bolus had hit a first-class 140 – and we were in a strong position. So I played a couple of overs and then thought I had to get as many runs as possible."

Everyone who ever played cricket with Garry Sobers during his 20-year career attests to his good nature, his complete lack of side. He may have stood head and shoulders above his Nottinghamshire team-mates but he afforded them respect at all times. From experienced professionals to new-comers to the side, everyone was treated in the same way.

"Garry was a gentleman who never belittled anybody he played with," recalls Frost. "He was the star man, he was paid star money but he didn't shove it down your throat. He basically just wanted to be one of the team – and he was."

"He had faith in the other players," confirms Bolus. "He never said he wouldn't be putting on someone because they couldn't bowl. He was Christian in his attitude."

It is therefore not surprising that Sobers should decline to point the finger at some of his team-mates for what other people have perceived as their pedestrian approach to batting in Nottinghamshire's first innings. Tony Lewis, writing in his 1985 autobiography, *Playing Days*, claimed that "it would have been a quiet sort of day if it had not been for one or two middle-order players, generous not to name, who sensed a declaration coming from their captain and selfishly blocked to make sure they would not be out and so improve their personal batting averages. They were using up valuable time."

Lewis then described his opposing skipper as "furious" as he came down the steps at the fall of fifth wicket. "A benign Sobers is not an animal to taunt," he wrote, "and a mad Sobers is a species to be avoided."

Forty years on, Lewis is prepared to name names or rather a name – that of one of Nottinghamshire's most reliable and consistent performers.

"The key to Sobers' performance that day," says Lewis, "was that Mike Smedley took an inordinate amount of time to get 20-odd and that really annoyed Garry who was looking to declare earlier."

There is little doubt that after he had understandably played second fiddle to Bolus, Smedley's partnership of 19 runs in 15 minutes with John Parkin put a brake on Nottinghamshire's charge towards a declaration. With more than a little help from White and Frost, Bolus had been the mainstay of the innings – *Wisden* described his century as "magnificent" – but the pace had slackened once he was out. But Smedley, who finished his 15-year career at Trent Bridge with a batting average of just over 31, remains unrepentant:

"I must admit that my knock that day is a bit of a blur," says Smedley, "but it was probably a little slow compared with the rest our innings. To me, scoring 27 in 40 minutes wasn't too bad. It's all in the context of the game. We had done pretty well so far and we thought we didn't need to lose wickets quickly. I don't think any of us scored particularly slowly during the day and it meant that at 308 for five, Garry could throw the bat at the ball with very little pressure to succeed. We were in such a good position and he was the icing on the cake, so to speak. If he got out straightaway, it wasn't any great problem – we'd still be ending up with a decent score. It was a small ground and Glamorgan had some decent Test players so we felt we needed to get a large total if we were going to win the game. I don't know which batsmen were playing for their averages but I wasn't one of them. I would have liked to have scored more runs but at the end of the day it was the team effort that mattered."

Whatever the motivation for Sobers' subsequent onslaught, the run rate certainly picked up as the tea interval approached. In the 11 minutes before the break, he scored 25 runs with Parkin adding two as Nottinghamshire moved to 335 for five. Sobers had been particularly harsh on Walker by hitting him for 15 – including a six and two fours – in the penultimate over of the afternoon session. "I wasn't surprised when Garry hammered me for six because he was a very good straight hitter," says the former all-rounder.

As he watched in wonder from the mid-wicket boundary, off-spinner Brian Lewis was, for once, delighted not to have been recalled to the Glamorgan attack.

"It wasn't so much the six sixes but the innings before them that impressed me," he says. "A lot of the runs Garry scored before that over had come down to me on the boundary. I managed to stop some of them – the ones and twos – but their power was immense. He hit the ball so effortlessly but it was like a brick coming towards you."

As Nash walked off the field for a well deserved cup of tea and a sandwich, he could justifiably reflect on a job well done. His bowling experiment had captured four wickets and although Sobers had scored two fours off his first over, he had only managed a single off each of his next two. On his arrival in the visitors' dressing room, the Nottinghamshire skipper decided to consult his troops about the timing of the impending declaration.

"At tea, Garry asked us how many runs we thought we wanted," says Bolus. "I said we didn't want too many; we didn't want to be in the same position as Hampshire were in our last match at Portsmouth. They had batted on too long – Barry Richards making 206 out of a first innings total of

411 – and they set us a target of 302 to win and the game ended in a draw."

During the tea interval, two other important discussions took place between BBC employees in London, Cardiff and Swansea. Live pictures of the game had been transmitted throughout the day to BBC Wales viewers via a two-camera unit perched precariously on some scaffolding behind and slightly to the left of the batsman at the Mumbles Road End. Commentary had been provided by Wilf Wooller, 'Mr Glamorgan', who had led the county to their first championship win in 1948 and was now serving the club as secretary. During the afternoon, the unit, with Bill Dyer on the locked-off camera and John Lewis manning the one that followed the ball, was placed on stand-by by *Grandstand* in London. At about twenty to five, BBC Wales director John Norman received a call via talkback from the programme's producer, Brian Venner, as he sat in the outside broadcast scanner at St Helen's.

"Brian said we were no longer needed and we might as well go home," said Norman, shortly before he died in July 2008. "As I prepared to close down, John Lewis, a keen cricketer, asked me if we could keep the scanner alive so he could watch Sobers bat through a fixed lens."

"Sobers was about to come in after tea," Lewis recalled, shortly before his death in 2006, "and I wanted to keep recording for a while to see how he did. Being a cricket enthusiast myself, I wanted to see him bat and follow his innings through my viewfinder. He was obviously a great player and I'd not seen him in the flesh before. I had no idea he was going to score six sixes but I thought he would have a good knock and hit a few balls around so we would enjoy his innings."

"Having heard London say they didn't need us in Swansea anymore," said Norman, "our recording engineer in Cardiff, Derek Griffin, could really have been expected to pack up and go home. He had no interest at all in sport, he started recording when you said 'start' and stopped when you said 'stop' and on this particular occasion, he kept recording."

Another stroke of good luck ensured that the BBC's output from St Helen's actually arrived in Cardiff where it was recorded by Griffin on that historic Saturday. "Because of the geography between Swansea and Cardiff," recalls Onllwyn Brace, the then BBC Wales head of sport who was also working as a director at the ground, "the pictures in those days had to be beamed back via a mid-link van with a signal relay dish on top which was parked on a mountain overlooking Maesteg. Fortunately, the man operating the link didn't decide to call it a day when we had been stood down by London. He could quite easily have hopped in his van and driven home so it was the result of a double dose of good fortune that we were recording that part of the game – it was a sheer fluke."

Norman had already been involved in the capture on videotape of a sensational sporting event when, nearly a year earlier, he was working for *Grandstand* in London on another rather quiet Saturday afternoon. The BBC were covering the Dunlop Masters golf tournament at Royal St George's at Sandwich in Kent in which an up-and-coming British player, the 23-year-old Tony Jacklin, was competing.

"I was looking after the videotape machines," recalled Norman, "and one of the operators said he wasn't recording anything at that time. I suggested we should record some golf and, quite by chance, I managed to catch Tony's hole-in-one on the 16th – it was the first time such a feat had been televised."

After landing, Jacklin's ball bounced a couple of times and then disappeared – to the sound of a great roar from the watching crowd. That ace at the par-three hole enabled Jacklin to complete a winning final round of 64 and launched his career in America, as well as kickstarting the process that led to European victories in the Majors, the Ryder Cup and the creation of today's European Tour.

"Recording Tony's shot was a great fluke," said Norman who, on that day at St Helen's in Swansea, had decided to have a quick word with the final member of his team – commentator Wooller, who had been involved with the BBC Wales coverage of Glamorgan's games since the early 1960s.

"It was hard work," recalled Wooller, two years before his death in 1997, "but I thoroughly enjoyed doing them although it meant that at certain matches I would be commentating, writing for *The Sunday Telegraph* and, as secretary, dealing with the mundane matters of making sure the toilets were clean and the scorecards were up to date."

Wooller was about to find himself caught up with an anything-but-mundane matter as the BBC team settled down to record the anticipated prelude to a long-awaited declaration. Through his headphones, Wooller received the instructions from Norman that would eventually send his voice resonating around the world.

"'If we're keeping running,' I said to Wilf, 'you might as well pick up the commentary – the news department might get something out of this for their Monday night programme.' But I had no idea what it was going to be!"

With the tea interval completed, Sobers and Parkin came down the flight of concrete steps and headed for the middle. The first over after tea was bowled by the recalled Don Shepherd from the Mumbles Road End but after hitting his first ball for a single, Sobers then had to stand and watch in frustration as Parkin failed to score off the next five. Sobers took three runs from the first two balls of Nash's over before Parkin entered into the party spirit by hitting his first boundary off the last ball. A tight over from Shepherd kept Sobers quiet until the last ball when he pinched a single and then nicked another run off Nash to give the strike to Parkin. Warming to his task, the number six smashed his second boundary.

"I can remember hitting that four over extra cover off Malcolm in the over before the famous one," says Parkin, "and immediately thinking: 'I'm getting into this now!' Then Garry scored nine off Don's next over – including a single to keep the bowling – and we had a chat in the middle at the end of it. We were 368 for five. I had 15 and Garry had made 40.

"'We'll have another 10 minutes,' Garry said.

"Fair enough, I thought, I'll have a go when I get down there – but I never got a chance!"

At about five minutes past five, Nash was preparing to bowl his 21st over of the match. Although wicketless since his 16th, he had produced a tidy spell of Underwood-style spinners and his four wickets had now cost him 64 runs. As he walked back to his mark, Nash had no idea that his next over would be the last in the Nottinghamshire innings – or the most well-known of his career. His next six deliveries would put his name up in lights and propel it into the history books forever.

The Big-Hitters Brigade (clockwise from top left)...
Ted Alletson, Cyril Smart, 'Big Jim' Smith and Arthur Wellard

Garry Sobers in England... with the touring West Indies in 1963 and after
signing for Nottinghamshire five years later

Sobersmania breaks out in Newark

In action against Worcestershire at New Road in June 1968...

...and in the six sixes match against Glamorgan in Swansea two months later

An aerial view of St Helen's where history was nearly made in 1967...

...when Glamorgan's Roger Davis was hit for five sixes in an over by Pakistan's Majid Khan

Glamorgan 1968 Back row (left to right): Graham Kingston,
Malcolm Nash, Eifion Jones, Roger Davis, Ian Morris,
Tony Cordle, Brian Lewis, Majid Khan, Kevin Lyons.
Front row: Alan Rees, Alan Jones, Don Shepherd, Tony Lewis
(captain), Peter Walker and Jeff Jones; and [inset] Ossie Wheatley

Nottinghamshire 1968 Back row: Deryck Murray, Mike Smedley,
Ian Moore, Dave Halfyard, Mike Taylor, Bob White, Graham Frost.
Front row: Norman Hill, Garry Sobers (captain), Brian Bolus and Carlton Forbes

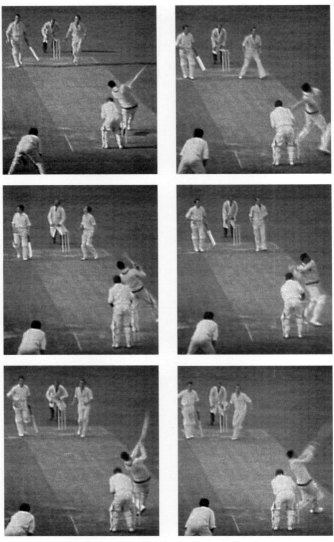

The six sixes... shot by shot (from top, left to right)

The 'catch' by Roger Davis off the fifth ball... six or out? (see overleaf)

Roger doesn't know if he has crossed the line... but umpire Eddie Phillipson eventually decides he has

As Malcolm Nash's last ball disappears "way down to Swansea", Sobers acknowledges the applause... before "the vanquished and the victor" face interviewer Brian Hoey and the BBC Wales cameras

Time		BATSMEN	RUNS AS SCORED
IN	OUT		
11.30	4.00	J.J. BOLUS	2212244WWll. 31/111.1|b|11 434 b141w1lij 11W14H 4W1b6ll6|e1 6 Sixes 18 fours
11.30	1.30	R. WHITE.	424Wl1|214 221W1 11WWl1 W1121W21 112l|122 9 fours
1.31	3.37	G. FROST	22W1221W11 11W121 421|6W1 15 ... 6 fours
3.38	4.18	M. SMEDLEY.	1W1311124 4WW
4.01	4.02	D. MURRAY	
4.03		J. PARKIN'	2122WH
4.19		G. SOBERS	WW1W6l41 112111441 666666. 15 ... 6 fours
		B. BRIGLEY (BRIGLEY)	

Look in the book: six sixes make cricket history

Boy returns six-hit ball

By J. B. G. THOMAS

Schoolboy Richard Lewis gave away his most prized possession yesterday . . . just 40 hours after he found it in a South Wales street.

It was the ball Gary Sobers thrashed for six consecutive sixes for a world record at St. Helen's, Swansea.

Richard, aged 17, a pupil at Pontardawe Grammar School, handed the ball to the Nottinghamshire captain at a ceremony in the St. Helen's pavilion.

The ball will now go on display at Trent Bridge—autographed by Sobers.

Temptation

Richard and his father, Mr. Charles Lewis, of High Street, Pontardawe, were watching the match on Saturday when Sobers hit his record-breaking 6's.

They left to go home for tea and found the ball outside the ground in St. Helen's Road. Mr. Lewis and Richard took it home and held a family conference to decide what to do with it.

"Although the temptation to keep the ball was great, we decided it should go back

to its proper place with Garfield Sobers," said Mr. Lewis.

"Still, we will treasure the fact that for a few hours we were in possession of the ball.

"Sobers is a great cricketer and it's only right that his feat should be remembered in this manner."

Try to win

Sobers said yesterday, "I never play cricket for records. I always go out to enjoy myself and try to win if possible, and the records created are just one of those things."

The ball may now become the world's second most famous cricket ball — behind the one which Jim Laker used to take 19 wickets against Australia at Old Trafford in 1956.

● Jeff Jones comeback?— Page 10.

Richard Lewis, aged 17, of Pontardawe, returns the cricket ball to Gary Sobers at St. Helen's yesterday.

Schoolboy Richard Lewis does the decent thing
and returns the ball two days later

Bowling seam rather than spin, Nash took nearly
1,000 first-class wickets in his 17 years with Glamorgan

Nash the Bash... hitting a century before lunch in a career-best
score of 130 against Middlesex at Lord's in April 1976

The other members of the Six Sixes Club... Ravi Shastri, who performed his feat on the way to scoring the fastest ever double century for Bombay against Baroda in 1985, and later became a well-respected television commentator

South Africa's Herschelle Gibbs claims his place in history against the Netherlands in the 2007 World Cup

Six months later, India's Yuvraj Singh scores the fastest international fifty in just 12 balls against England in the Twenty20 World Cup

Coach Nash and ICC ambassador Sobers back together in 2000 for the first
Under-13 game between the United States and Canada

Thanks boys... Garry Sobers at St Helen's in 2006 with the men who preserved
his performance for posterity... director John Norman (left) and cameraman
John Lewis (right), both of whom have since passed away

'Was it still rolling?....the superstar and the schoolboy swap memories of the lost-and-found ball at a six sixes dinner in June 2008

The bat and the ball... the Slazenger short-handled bat fetched £54,000 at auction in 2000 and the ball went for £26,400 in 2006

Forty years on... the not-so-famous
five who provided the platform for
The Great Man... (from top, left to
right) Bob White, Brian Bolus,
Graham Frost, Mike Smedley and
John Parkin, the not-out batsman

And (opposite and overleaf) the
Glamorgan fielders who could only
stand and stare... Alan Jones, Roger
Davis, Majid Khan, Tony Lewis,
Peter Walker and Tony Cordle

Malcolm Nash, Brian Lewis, Don
Shepherd, Ossie Wheatley, who went
off injured, and his replacement,
twelfth man Alan Rees

THE FIRST BALL

Malcolm Andrew Nash was really pleased with the nickname he was given by his new Glamorgan team-mates. Because his initials were M.A.N. and he was very sure of himself, they just put a 'super' on the front. Of course, he knew they were poking fun at him – leg-pulling is an integral ingredient in creating team spirit in any dressing room – but he was chuffed, almost flattered, to receive such a moniker. Some people called him cocky; others thought he was arrogant. He felt the nickname accurately reflected his attitude towards the game.

He may not have looked or behaved like the mild-mannered Clark Kent – and he certainly didn't own a costume with the familiar "S" insignia in the centre of it – but when the Glamorgan bowler donned his whites and walked out on to a cricket field with a ball in his hand, he felt that anything was possible: nothing was beyond him.

The trouble was that during a five-minute spell on Saturday 31st August 1968, Malcolm 'Superman' Nash met his match when he ran into the genuine article – a real-life superhero with superhuman powers in the shape of Garfield St Auburn Sobers. And, as history shows, in the battle between a man who thought he could do anything and one who could do virtually everything, there was only going to be one winner.

Nash's inherent belief in his own ability was a fundamental part of his make-up. Without it, and his knack of swinging the ball both into and away from opposing batsmen, he would not have taken nearly 1,000 wickets in a first-class career spanning 17 years.

"Most people in the side used to call me 'Superman' because of my initials and I admit I was very self-confident," he recalls. "When Garry came in to bat at St Helen's, I was excited because it was the first time I had come up against him – our match at Trent Bridge earlier in the season had been abandoned without a ball being bowled. I wanted to bowl at someone who I thought was the best player in the world so it didn't give me any problems mentally. I just set about the business of trying to get him out. I never changed my ideas and thoughts about what I was trying to do."

"Malcolm was always very confident," recalls skipper Tony Lewis, "and that was part of his skill. He always wanted to bowl and sometimes I had to tear the ball out of his hands to get him off. He was a dangerous man with the new ball and he could swing it for a long time during an innings."

When he came up against Sobers at St Helen's, Nash was barely two years into his Glamorgan career. Before joining the county, he had turned out for his home town club of Abergavenny during the summer holidays and also played hockey for Wales at Under-23 level. He made his first-class debut against Cambridge University in June 1966 when he took two for 30 in a drawn match.

In 1967, Nash became a semi-regular in the county side. The England Test player, Jeff Jones, and Tony Cordle normally opened the bowling and Nash, after picking up the odd wicket here and there, took a season's best of six for 44 against Sussex at Hove in his fourth game before ending up with 24 wickets in 18 matches at an average of 30.45.

But the summer of 1968 was to transform his career. It could hardly have started any better for him because in Glamorgan's first championship game against Gloucestershire at Lydney, Nash took six for 25 from 17 overs. When Jones suffered what turned out to be career-ending shoulder and elbow injuries against Essex at Ilford in early June, Nash found himself sharing new-ball duties with Cordle more often. He seized his opportunity by turning in his best performance of the season in an amazing game at St

Helen's in the middle of July when he picked up 10 wickets in a match for the first time. After taking three for 57 in Somerset's first innings, Nash helped to ensure that no batsman reached double figures when Somerset batted again and Glamorgan cruised to an easy win.

"Somerset must have wondered how they lost this game," recorded *Wisden*. "They were leading by 133 runs on the first innings, but a magnificent spell of swing bowling by the 23-year-old Nash completely transformed the picture late on the second day when Somerset, batting a second time, were tumbled out for 40. Nash had the following remarkable analysis – 13.3 overs, 7 maidens, 15 runs, 7 wickets. This, on the same pitch on which Somerset scored 337 in their first innings, was incredible. Kitchen, Chappel and Palmer had batted so soundly that Somerset's subsequent collapse was inexplicable. The pitch had not deteriorated in any way and this was emphasised when Glamorgan, needing 174 to win, got their runs for the loss of only one wicket."

"I guess it was part of my learning curve," Nash recalls. "It confirmed the belief that Wilf Wooller, Ossie Wheatley and Tony Lewis had in me and my ability to swing the ball in late. I never doubted my own ability: I always believed I could get people out, no matter who I played against. If you don't have that mind-set, you shouldn't be playing. You must accept the challenge to perform to the levels that other people believe you can."

"I think Malcolm was a very fine bowler for the county," says Majid Khan, who took one of five catches in Nash's seven-wicket haul against Somerset. "Any swing bowler troubles batsmen and Malcolm kept troubling them because he would bring the ball in and then have one which went away so they were kept guessing. And that was basically his strength. If you can swing the ball both ways, you have much more chance against any batsman than if you just bowl straight up and down."

After dismissing just one Northamptonshire batsman in a win at Kettering, Nash was back among the wickets in Glamorgan's next match against Warwickshire at Edgbaston. He took three for 52 and five for 71 as the county won by 30 runs. But his personal highlight of the 1968 season came just over three weeks before the Nottinghamshire match when, for the second consecutive time, Glamorgan beat the Australians – again at St Helen's. After bowling out the Welsh side for 224, the tourists were dismissed for 110 – with Nash producing another devastating spell to finish with five for 28 from 15.3 overs.

"That was brilliant bowling," recalls stand-in skipper Don Shepherd, who took a record 2,174 wickets during his 22-year Glamorgan career. "He was left-arm over the wicket and by no means quick but he had that little bit of zip off the pitch which some bowlers have and some don't. Malcolm could duck the ball into and across the right-hander and I would suggest that his strike rate with the new ball was probably as good as anyone who was playing at the time."

"It was a very exciting three days," recalls Nash. "I had moved up another level to international cricket and there's nothing like being involved in the big occasion – there was lots of noise and excitement all through the game and everyone was asking, after our 1964 win, if we could do it again. A couple of my wickets – like John Gleeson and Alan Connolly – were tailenders but Bob Cowper and Ian Redpath were good names. I'm not a great stats man but it was certainly a great feeling to pick up a fifer."

Nash took another wicket in Australia's second innings as Glamorgan pulled off another famous victory by 79 runs. Ten days before Nottinghamshire arrived at St Helen's, he returned figures of three for eight in a 10-wicket win over Surrey at Neath as Glamorgan maintained their challenge for the championship but only dismissed two batsmen when Welsh hopes of lifting the title were finally dashed by a defeat by Derbyshire in Cardiff.

While Nash was making his mark during the 1968 season, Ossie Wheatley had been enjoying an Indian summer – at the precise moment when he was winding down his career. The injury to Jones at Ilford which ruled him out for the rest of the season meant that 33-year-old Wheatley found himself having to unpack his kitbag for what he imagined would almost certainly be a last hurrah. The former Warwickshire fast-medium bowler had been a key Glamorgan player since joining the club as successor to the legendary Wilf Wooller as captain in 1961. The county's historian, Dr. Andrew Hignell, has described Wheatley's leadership as "a mix of good humour and debonair authority" and it was certainly different.

"In a funny way, Wilf was a hard act to follow and he wasn't," reflects Wheatley. "Obviously, he was extremely well-known, a very strong character and, in some ways, my appointment was greeted with relief – by the players, in the sense that my regime was likely to be kinder to them, and by other sides who had suffered at the wrong end of Wilf's tongue from time to time. They would all find it easier to negotiate with me – it's probably best to put it that way.

"I was a great believer in enjoying cricket and in people practising and honing up their skills. I inherited a side which was about to lose three quite distinguished players – Gilbert Parkhouse, Allan Watkins and Jim McConnon – and therefore we started off with a relatively young team which was very much easier to handle than the old timers who are set in their ways. I think the new players were reasonably pleased to see me. I was a new broom. I enjoyed captaincy very much and I don't think I probably would have played on as long as I did if I hadn't been captain. It was much more interesting being in charge of the team and making sure we had decent games of cricket."

Wheatley took 100 wickets in his first two seasons with Glamorgan and under his leadership, they normally finished in the bottom half of the table. But the county hinted at the success they would achieve later in the decade by coming second in 1963 and third in 1965 and in between, Wheatley led them to a 36-run victory over the Australian tourists at St Helen's. They slipped back to 14th in 1966 as he again collected 100 wickets before being succeeded by Tony Lewis who, after a disappointing first season, led a strong challenge for the title in 1968.

"I'd virtually packed up in 1966 and I played only four championship games when I wasn't very fit in 1967," he recalls. "I then decided I would get fit and played a few pre-season and early-season games for St Fagans, near Cardiff, in 1968. They were good enough to let me bowl a lot so when I came into the Glamorgan side in early June, partly because Jeff Jones was injured, I was actually cricket-fit."

On his return to the first team, Wheatley produced a remarkable purple patch which would lead to him being chosen as one of *Wisden's* Cricketers of the Year. Three wickets against Sussex at Hove meant he collected 1,000 in his career, he took seven for 45 against Northampton at St Helen's and then seven for 51 in another draw against Gloucestershire in Cardiff.

"It was the first time I'd played regularly since I'd stopped being captain," says Wheatley, "and I suppose I was able to focus on my own performance that bit more. It was a nice opportunity and it made the point that if you didn't play quite as much cricket as a bowler, you were much fitter towards the end of the season and could carry on right through to the end of August. By the time you'd bowled 800 or 900 or even 1,000 overs in a season, you were actually knackered by then. It worked to my advantage."

When Kent came to St Helen's in late June, the former captain picked up six for 67 and a month later crowned an incredible comeback when Sussex were swept away at Ebbw Vale in Glamorgan's fourth successive win.

"After obtaining a substantial first-innings lead of 117 through another sound century by Alan Jones," recorded *Wisden*, "Glamorgan never relaxed their grip on the game and an innings victory was assured by the magnificent bowling of Wheatley when Sussex batted a second time. He took the first seven wickets that fell at a personal cost of 33 runs and, claiming the extra half hour, Glamorgan tried to win in two days. Lewis and Bates, however, held out, although on the final morning Wheatley soon captured the remaining wickets to finish with nine for 60 – his best analysis in first-class cricket. Since joining the side in an emergency owing to the injury to Jeff Jones, Wheatley's record was 43 wickets in eight matches and his bowling was a big factor in Glamorgan's revival."

And it didn't end there. As Glamorgan kept up the pressure on the championship pace-setters, Yorkshire, Wheatley collected nine wickets against Lancashire, six in a win over Surrey, seven against Somerset and five against Derbyshire.

It was perhaps no surprise that Wheatley's workload would eventually take its toll. As Nash was preparing to send down the first ball of the 99th over to Garry Sobers at St Helen's, his opening partner had been forced off the field. After bowling a wicketless five overs for 22 runs, Wheatley was taking a well-earned rest – as far away from the action as he could possibly be.

"In those days, there were seats right up alongside the roof at the very top of the pavilion so I went to sit up there and was looking down on the whole thing," he recalls. "It was a great spectacle because I had a bird's eye view from that height – unusually high. My sore shins had been caused by bowling a lot of overs in a fairly short time and the problem had been building up. It was quite a good time for Malcolm to try out his spinners: it was pretty certain that Notts were going to declare, the conditions were dry and it was a batter's wicket."

Wheatley's place in the field after lunch had been filled for the first half hour by the former Welsh footballer, Trevor

Ford who began his professional career at Swansea and went on to play for Aston Villa and Sunderland before returning to Wales with Cardiff City and then having a brief spell with PSV Eindhoven in Holland and Newport County. He won 38 caps for Wales and scored a then-record 23 goals. In his youth, Ford had played for Welsh schoolboys at cricket alongside Welsh international footballer, Alf Sherwood, and Glamorgan's Gilbert Parkhouse. In the absence of an official twelfth man, the Swansea-born centre-forward had volunteered to help out before a call to the home of Alan Rees at nearby Port Talbot ended Ford's brief sojourn in the sun.

Rees was a right-hand middle-order bat, a seam bowler and a superb fielder who had made his county debut against Somerset at Weston-super-Mare in 1955. He was short, had a low centre of gravity and was an instinctive ball player with a pair of good hands.

"Ever since I was a kid, the one thing I could do was run and catch a ball," says Rees. "I fielded in the covers and at mid-wicket – where I picked up a lot of wickets for Don Shepherd because batsmen would try to flick him away.

"I was sitting watching television when the phone went on that Saturday. It was somebody from Glamorgan who told me to get down to Swansea with my kit because I was needed in the field. I must admit that I never felt part of the team that day – simply because I was twelfth man. I wasn't cheesed off about being called up but I was unhappy because I knew by then that my contract wasn't going to be renewed. I think we'd been playing at Cardiff when I was told I was being released – I wouldn't be required for the 1969 season. Something was said about a summer contract for the John Player League which was just starting – I might be needed because of injuries. I'd been in and out of the side, I only played in 13 of the 28 championship matches and scored just over 300 runs so, to be fair, I suppose I hadn't had a very remarkable season. The funny part about it was that I thought I had the best chance of hitting some form in the one-day game. It would have suited me fine and I could have turned my arm over a bit with my weekend seamers."

Rees had established himself as a regular in the Glamorgan side in the late 1950s just as his burgeoning rugby union career was starting to take off. He played at fly-half for Maesteg, Aberavon and Llanelli and won three Welsh caps in 1962 before turning professional and joining the Leeds rugby league team for £6,000 at the end of that season.

"Making my debut for Wales at Twickenham was the highlight of my sporting career," recalls Rees. "It was a terrible game which ended 0-0 but I kicked a drop goal against Scotland in my second match and then I played against France."

While with Llanelli, Rees partnered scrum-half Onllwyn Brace who won nine Welsh caps between 1956 and 1961 before becoming head of sport at BBC Wales in Cardiff.

"You could throw anything at Alan and he'd catch it," recalls Brace. "His cricketing reactions served him well on the rugby field. In fact, he was one of the best fly-halves, if not the best, that I played with, in that he suited a scrum-half perfectly. He was quick on his feet – and tremendously quick off the mark – he had perfect hands and he could kick with either foot. In many ways, he had all the virtues of a great fly-half. From a scrum-half's point of view, I would rate him as a wonderful partner."

"There are two things I regret when I look back at my life," reflects Rees. "One was going north and the other was not making myself available for the British Lions tour to South Africa in the summer of 1962. After my first international, letters were sent out to all the players asking about their availability but I was contracted and getting paid by Glamorgan so I couldn't automatically say I was OK to go. In my lack of wisdom possibly, I never went to Wilf Wooller or Ossie to discuss it. They both said to me later that I could have had a year out and gone on the tour. It would have been the highlight of my career. I regret going north because I didn't like the game – I never fitted in. I ended up on the touchline ever time I bloody played. I was knocked out! Whoosh! bang! a stiff arm on my nose! It's not very straight now and I've had it straightened supposedly. Rugby league wasn't for me."

It was while he was playing for Leeds that Rees came across Garry Sobers for the first time on a cricket field. The West Indies were touring England in 1963 and in early June they arrived at Cardiff Arms Park where Glamorgan used to play their matches in the capital until 1967. After being bowled out for 163 – with Sobers taking four wickets and Rees making 29 not out – Glamorgan were being put to the sword when Sobers came in at number five. It was a short innings because Rees ran him out for a duck.

"I remember him hitting the ball and shouting 'come one!'" says Rees. "The ball came straight to me: bang! wickets down! thank you! I was really loved that day mind you. The crowd didn't want to see me field, they wanted to see Sobers bat. I wasn't very popular, there were a few choice remarks made in jest but nothing serious because we had got The Great Man out. It's a very fond memory that I cherish."

His reputation as one of the best cover points in the game led in 1964 to Rees making the first of two memorable appearances as a substitute fielder. England were playing Australia in the third Test at Headingley when the disgruntled rugby league player was told by Wilf Wooller to head off to Leeds. Rees had just scored 56 in a drawn game against Middlesex in Cardiff and took the place of the injured Worcestershire bowler, Jack Flavell, as Australia reached 389 all out on the Saturday.

"I was fielding at deep mid-wicket when I caught Peter Burge for 160 off Fred Trueman," he recalls. "Fred dropped one short, Peter smacked it high towards me and I had to run along the boundary and take it as it was coming down. Anytime you take a catch is great but I felt on top of the world with this one: a Yorkshire crowd in Leeds with Fred, the idol of the North, bowling – it was fantastic.

"'I trapped him," said Fred when he came over to thank me. 'I knew you were out there so I dropped it short and let him hook.'

"Peter was 160 not out at the time and his was the last wicket to fall so I don't think Fred trapped him really!"

In truth, Trueman had not been at his best at Headingley – bowling far too short at Burge with the second new ball – but the Australian became his 296th Test victim. Although he picked up another wicket in the second innings, Trueman was then dropped for the fourth Test at Old Trafford in Manchester before being recalled for the final Test at The Oval when he reached the 300-wicket milestone.

"Taking the catch was a great moment for me but it was great just being on the field," says Rees. "The atmosphere was so different. When Glamorgan beat the Australians in 1964 and 1968, the atmosphere at St Helen's was electric but just walking out with the England team to field, with no Glamorgan sweater on because it was so hot, was something else."

Two weeks later, Rees finally scored his first century for Glamorgan – before making a second in the very next match. He hit 106 not out against Kent in Maidstone to beat his previous top score of 95 and then immediately re-wrote his own personal record book with an unbeaten knock of 111 against Lancashire in Cardiff.

"I was in the side mainly for my batting and a hundred was a magical figure that you strived for so when the moment arrived, it felt marvellous," Rees recalls. "At Maidstone, we were fighting a rearguard action because we'd been stuffed out of sight early on and Jim Pressdee and I batted for most of the last day to secure a draw. We came together at 135 for five and we finished up on 342. 'Pres', who made 97 not out, was his usual stubborn self and I just managed to get to three figures. I scored nearly 1,000 championship runs, and more than 1,200 in all competitions, in that season."

A fortnight later, Rees played a key part in Glamorgan's victory over the Australians at Swansea. He top scored with 48 and 47 in both innings and took the crucial catch to dismiss skipper Bill Lawry as the tourists chased 269 to win. The Australian captain had dropped anchor and *Wisden* reported that "Hour after hour, he defied the Glamorgan bowlers in a dour but dedicated innings of intense concentration. As long as he stayed, his side looked like winning."

After batting for nearly five hours for 64 runs, Lawry hit a Pressdee long hop in the meat of the bat through midwicket where Rees took a stunning head-high catch to make it 207 for six. Australia were all out for 232.

"The ball was motoring," says Rees. "It came like a rocket and although I saw it, my movements were pure reflex. It was one of the worst balls 'Pres' ever bowled and it had 'six' written all over it. But that's cricket – it's not always the good balls that get you out. It was a more important catch than the Headingley one because England weren't going to win that game. Up until Lawry was out, we were losing the game."

The following year saw Rees end his connection with rugby league and concentrate on his cricket career. During a championship match against Middlesex at Lord's in August, he had the rare and notorious distinction of being dismissed "handled ball". It was only the second time such an event had occurred since the county championship had been officially constituted in 1890. Charles Wright was out in the same way while playing for Nottinghamshire against Gloucestershire at Bristol in 1893.

"We were chasing 286 to win on the final day," recalls Rees. "It was nip and tuck and Freddie Titmus was bowling when we started to get behind. I got a little frustrated and I charged him. He saw me coming and flipped it down my leg side, slightly quicker. I was caught out of my ground and as the ball went past me, I took my hand off the bat handle and, in a reflex action, caught the ball cleanly, dropped it and then walked back to my crease. Ron Aspinall was the umpire at square leg and he and the other umpire, John Arnold, were both perplexed – they didn't know what the hell to do! There seemed to be a pause and then a very calm appeal from Freddie, the Middlesex captain. 'Howzat?' The two umpires came together to have a little chat and John said to me: 'I'm afraid Alan, you're out' – but very sympathetically. The ball wasn't going to hit the wicket but I probably would have been stumped. I wasn't thinking about that though: it happened too quickly for that. It was a straight reflex action."

Having been summoned to St Helen's for Glamorgan's 1968 match against Nottinghamshire, Rees realised he would be spending a long afternoon in the field. Despite having lost a wicket, Nottinghamshire were still making the most of a good batting track, the runs were flowing freely and Garry Sobers was the star attraction for the Bank Holiday crowd.

"When I went on to the field, I could sense the anticipation from the crowd. They were waiting for Sobers to come in – as happens with all great cricketers. As a boy, I used to go down to see Glamorgan play against the three Ws – Everton Weekes, Frank Worrell and Clyde Walcott – for the West Indies as well as against Australians like Neil Harvey and it was a thrill to watch all the best players in the world. I was always a big admirer of Sobers."

Rees had been on the field for just over an hour when he caught Brian Bolus at mid-off to end Nottinghamshire's second-wicket partnership of 132 with the score on 289. Then Deryck Murray came and went very quickly to be followed by Mike Smedley, John Parkin and eventually, when Smedley was out, by the Nottinghamshire captain.

"After tea," recalls Rees, "Sobers just hit everything. We

were looking for Notts to get some runs on the board so we could get out to bat. The rest of the Glamorgan team had had a long day in the field and couldn't wait to get off. To be fair, 'Nashy' wasn't a spinner – although he always had an inkling to be one – but he was a good fast-medium swing bowler."

Up on the pavilion roof, Ossie Wheatley, out of the line of fire, was sympathising with his team-mates as they toiled in the August Bank Holiday sun – secretly happy to be watching the match from the sidelines. By this time, the field placings had inevitably changed. Skipper Tony Lewis was at mid-off, Roger Davis at long-off, Don Shepherd at short third man, Majid Khan at slip and, apart from wicket-keeper Eifion Jones, the rest of Glamorgan's players were patrolling the leg-side with its short boundary because the allocated strip for the match lay closer to the Gorse Lane side than the rugby pitch part of St Helen's. Familiar local landmarks such as The Cricketers pub, on the corner of King Edward's Road, and the scoreboard, not far from St Helen's Avenue, were about to become even more well known during the next five minutes.

Out on the square, Malcolm Nash was about to deliver the first ball of the 99th over from around the wicket at the Pavilion End. Just in front of him, umpire Eddie Phillipson was standing back, about three yards from the stumps, hands on knees, in a slightly crouched position. John Parkin, right glove on hip, prepared to move off as Nash, clasping the ball in both hands, began his run-up of no more than half a dozen paces.

"It was a challenge because I was playing against the best in the world and I just wanted to get Garry out," says Nash. "You do that by bowling straight and attacking the batsman. Unless he comes down the wicket and you beat him in the air and he gets stumped, you've either got to turn the ball enough for him to miss it or create an error on his part in order for him to mis-hit a ball."

At the other end, three men waited for his first delivery –

Eifion Jones, hoping for a nick outside the off stump, Majid Khan, hands on knees at slip and Garry Sobers, his mind made up.

"I was on 40 and thought I should go for it," he recalls. "There was a short boundary on the Gorse Lane side of the square, by the scorebox, and there was no risk if you really connected. I made up my mind to hit the ball over the boundary – irrespective of where it was pitched. My intention was to swing so hard at each ball that even a mis-hit would clear it.

"As Malcolm prepared to bowl, I remembered the two versions of how to get quick runs. Everton Weekes used to tell me that if I kept the ball on the ground no one could catch me while Sir Learie Constantine preferred the alternative, saying if you hit it up in the air and out of the ground nobody could catch it anyway. On that occasion, I chose the Lord Constantine version. Since my wicket was not an issue, I decided I was going to hit it in the air and take the risks. There were no thoughts of six sixes at that stage, just runs, and I was not even bothered whether I was out or not. All I was interested in was quick runs and a declaration."

As Nash arrived at the crease, the ball now firmly in his left hand, Parkin walked forward down the wicket alongside him while Jones and Majid dropped lower onto their haunches. Sobers stood motionless, apart from a single tap of his bat on the ground, until the ball left Nash's hand and landed in front of him. Thwack! A majestic swing of his Slazenger short-handled, four star blade, with the spin, launched the ball out of the ground, over the heads of Alan Rees at mid-wicket and then Tony Cordle at wide long-on. As it left the bat, Phillipson ducked slightly to his left, almost as if he thought it was, somehow, coming his way. He then turned to try to follow its path as the ball sailed past a floodlight pylon and hit the wall of The Cricketers pub before bouncing down into the road. As the spectators started to applaud,

Majid came in for a chat with Jones. Bat at the ready, Sobers stood to the right of the crease, grinning from ear to ear.

"When the first one went for six," says Wheatley, "I thought it was just routine. Fair enough, Sobers likes to whack the ball and St Helen's is a fairly tight ground."

"As the sixes started flying," recalls Rees, "I thought it was good entertainment. Malcolm wasn't bowling his usual style so it was a bit like playing in a benefit game where everybody would have a bowl and sixes and fours would be smacked around to entertain the crowd – it was Sunday afternoon cricket."

"I was looking to get down that end," says Parkin who immediately applauded the shot with his glove and bat. "I was keen to get on strike. As a young lad, I wanted to run, to be involved, but there was no chance of that happening."

"I was just concentrating like hell on what I had to do," said BBC Wales cameraman John Lewis. "My job was to follow the ball. I knew if I missed anything, there was absolutely no back-up."

In the commentary box, Wilf Wooller, with the help of scorer Bill Edwards, was starting to do his sums:

"He's hit that out of the ground – way up, many a mile, past the pylon there, over into the road, near the old Cricketers. He's smiling all over his face. The ball's been returned. Forty-six now to Sobers and he's been at the wicket for … how long, Bill Edwards?" Thirty minutes … so the fastest century is on."

Runs rather than records were on Garry Sobers' mind. Malcolm Nash was thinking about his next ball. One down, five to go.

THE SECOND BALL

When John Parkin became a professional cricketer by joining the Nottinghamshire ground staff in 1965, his parents gave him an autograph book to mark the achievement. Morris and Gladys Parkin were very proud of their 20-year-old son and they were obviously delighted when his native county decided to offer him a contract. When Parkin opened up the book, he found a good luck message from his parents in the form of a few lines of verse:

> John… someday you will make us proud
> As we sit among the crowd
> Watching you make the grade
> With ball or flashing blade.
> So play up and "play the game"
> And we can tell the folk your name.
> So always remember my lad
> There's two watching you – your Mam and Dad.

"That book – and especially the poem – is something I've treasured ever since," says Parkin, recently retired as a bricklayer and still living in his home village of Kimberley, near Nottingham. "My old man was as chuffed as mint balls that I'd got there. He wasn't a bad player himself, a good bowler, but he never told me about that. And he'd never tell me when he was coming to watch me play for the county. Even if I got a big score, it would always be the last ball – the bad shot that I got out with – that he'd talk to me about later. He wasn't one for giving out praise. But the autograph book spurred me on and when I pick it up now, more than 40 years later, it really gets to me."

The sad truth is though, as he himself readily admits, Parkin didn't make the grade – with either "ball or flashing blade" or with the pair of wicket-keeping gloves he used to don every now and then during his career as a county crick-eter. Parkin was a peripheral player, someone who, more often than not, was on the edge of the action, looking on – especially on that day when he became part of history at St Helen's in Swansea.

Parkin's was not the most auspicious entry into first-class cricket. He made his debut against Kent at Trent Bridge in May 1966 and, batting at number seven, failed to trouble the scorers. He made another nine championship appearances during the season and played two fewer games in 1967 when he scored 53 against Lancashire during a drawn match at Trent Bridge.

"That was my highest score for the first team which I was quite chuffed about because Brian Statham, Peter Lever and Barry Wood were bowling for them," says Parkin. "Statham had played for England and the other two would go on to in the next few years. I was bowled by Statham on a track that had some bounce in it and became one of his five wickets."

Parkin played his first game of the 1968 season as Derbyshire were beaten by three wickets at Trent Bridge in the middle of June when three players, including Garry Sobers, were rested. He was picked another seven times before disappearing back to the second team for most of August until being called up for the Glamorgan match.

"I'd been playing in a second-team match against Warwickshire at Leamington Spa when I got the message to go down to Swansea," recalls Parkin. "I scored seven and one batting at number four, we lost, and as far as I was con-cerned, the season was over. I couldn't understand my call-up because I'd had a poor season and for most of the time, I'd been in the seconds."

But injuries to two players gave him another chance in the first team and he travelled down to Swansea the day before the match began. Parkin's frank self-assessment of his career – "in my own mind, I wasn't quite good enough" – strikes a chord with other members of the Nottinghamshire side who faced Glamorgan in their last game of the 1968 season. By this time, Graham Frost had established himself as the first team's number three batsman, after coming through the ranks of schools, youth and county cricket in Nottinghamshire with Parkin. The pair lived in neighbouring villages and were sometimes mistaken for each other.

"John was a very correct batsman but quite a nervous fellow which is possibly why he didn't produce the goods at first-class level like he did in the seconds," says Frost. "He was a Kimberley lad through and through and I was from Basford, a couple of miles away, and we had a lot of battles together as we grew up. I didn't think I was top drawer. I was a good county player but I knew I wasn't going to make it as an international and I understand why John felt that he wasn't quite up to the county grade. Because we were similar in appearance, a lot of people used to stop me in the street thinking it was me who was batting with Garry during the six sixes so I had to put them straight on that. John was a really genuine, nice guy – one of the many that you meet in cricket."

"My bone of contention," says Parkin, "was that when I got in the side in 1966, there were 65 compulsory overs in the first innings and that didn't do me a lot of good because when I went in, we were either in trouble or having to get on with it."

"John's description of himself is accurate," recalls Brian Bolus, the former Nottinghamshire and England opening batsman. "He was a very successful club cricketer who played well in our second team and was given his opportunity in the firsts – more because other people didn't do well than him forcing his way in. Mind you, he was batting at six or seven and he was either going in when there was a crisis or quick runs were needed. It was an impossible position for a lad who was a down-the-middle, dead straight, decent batsman. He was a proper batter but he wasn't of the quality either to force his way in or, when he did get a chance, he couldn't impose himself because the circumstances were wrong for him. Like I couldn't cut it at Test level, John couldn't cut it at county level. Mind you, he's part of a great quiz question – who was batting at the other end when Garry Sobers scored his six sixes?"

Bob White could sympathise with Parkin's position at Trent Bridge because he had suffered a similar fate when playing for Middlesex during the first half of his career.

"Cricket's a bloody difficult game when you play every day," he says, "and I felt sorry for lads like John and Richard Bielby, the other late replacement at Swansea, because they only came in to the team now and again. They were good batsmen but they were on the fringe. I had the same problem at Lord's – I was under pressure the whole time. Because I was in and out, in and out with Middlesex, it knocked my confidence a bit. If we played Surrey, I'd be up against Alec Bedser, Peter May, Mickey Stewart and Ken Barrington and I'd stand there at the crease thinking: 'What the hell am I doing with this lot?'"

Frustrated and unsure of his future, Parkin was understandably short of confidence when he arrived at Swansea – and it showed. He pottered about the crease picking up ones and twos while batting with Smedley and was heartened by the arrival of his captain at about twenty past four. "Garry didn't say anything to me when he came in," he recalls. "I just let him get on with it."

Out on the mid-wicket boundary, another 23-year-old, Brian Lewis, had been growing more confident throughout that summer. After spending two years at Lord's as a young professional, the Maesteg-born off-spinner made his first-class debut in a 110-run win over Lancashire at St Helen's in 1965 without taking a wicket. He played four championship games in 1966, eight in 1967 and he finally made the breakthrough as the back-up spinner to the evergreen Don

Shepherd in 1968. In the middle of May, he took four for 46 in Hampshire's first innings in a two-wicket win at Southampton before returning a career-best seven for 28 when the home side batted again.

"I was a regular member of the team in 1968 but I'd been in and out before then," recalls Lewis. "Like all counties at that time, Glamorgan would bring you in for a game and if you didn't perform wonders straightaway, you were back out, then back in and then back out."

Roger Davis was an occasional off-spinner and contemporary of Lewis' after they had joined the Glamorgan groundstaff together in 1965. "Brian was a fantastic bowler because he really turned it – he was probably one of the biggest turners of a ball I've ever come across. He could bat a bit and he was a good slipper as well. He was a better off-spinner than me and he showed he had the potential to become a really good county bowler during that season."

A month before the Nottinghamshire match, Lewis announced his arrival on the big stage when he played a vital role in Glamorgan's second defeat of the Australians in four years. With a throat infection keeping out Tony Lewis, Shepherd took over as captain and after being bowled out for 224, Glamorgan made early inroads into the Australian batting line-up – first through Malcolm Nash and then Lewis. At the close of play on the first day, the tourists were 88 for six and were eventually dismissed for 110 with Lewis finishing with four for 51 from 20 overs. But it was his unbroken spell of 32 overs in the second innings, after Shepherd had set the Australians a target of 365 on the final day, which proved crucial. In trying to keep the tourists interested in winning, Shepherd made greater use of Lewis' off-breaks than of his own medium-paced variety.

"I don't want to be disrespectful to Brian," says Shepherd, "but he was a big spinner of the ball, he was learning his trade and he wasn't as accurate then. I kept fiddling with his field on the leg-side and it suited the team's purpose for him to pick up the occasional wicket and for Australia to get a few runs, to keep the scoreboard ticking over."

At 116 for two, Australia were going well but Bob Cowper and Les Joslin then fell to Lewis in the space of 10 balls and the young off-spinner later took the wicket of leg-break bowler John Gleeson to finish with three for 131 as the tourists were bowled out for 285.

"I had a good game against the Australians," recalls Lewis, modestly. "I suppose, along with Malcolm, who took six for 50 in the game, I was one of the match-winners. I remember, with a run-out, Malcolm and I were tied on four wickets each in their first innings and he managed to get his fifth one."

"In such a pressure cooker of an atmosphere," says all-rounder Peter Walker, "this was a commendable haul by a young and inexperienced bowler."

And to prove it wasn't a one-off, Lewis took five for 57 against Derbyshire at Derby, passed 50 wickets for the season when he picked up his only victim against Somerset at Taunton and then took four for 39 in the crucial defeat by Derby in Cardiff just before the six sixes game.

As Nottinghamshire piled on the runs at St Helen's, Lewis made the important breakthrough by taking the first wicket. He had Bob White caught by Ossie Wheatley near the beginning of a 13-over unbroken spell before being left to concentrate on his fielding for the rest of the innings.

But once Sobers had finally declared on 394 for five, Lewis found himself having to help Glamorgan avoid the follow-on in the middle of the afternoon of the second day. Alan Jones (25), Majid Khan (41) and Eifion Jones (29) had all made important contributions and Peter Walker was heading towards an unbeaten century. Batting at number nine, Lewis joined him when Nash, after hitting David Halfyard for six, was bowled, ironically, by Sobers with the score at 179 for eight. It looked all up for Glamorgan but Lewis had other ideas. His first scoring shot was a six off the bowling, of all people, the West Indian captain. As Alan Gibson of *The Times* reported, "Lewis began by attacking fiercely. He hit Sobers for 14 in three consecutive balls which delighted the crowd, as some repayment for the indignities of the previous day."

John Billot, writing in the *Western Mail*, was also full of praise for Lewis who, he said, "became Glamorgan's answer to Sobers. Brian batted like Tony Lewis – in fact, rather better than his captain in this innings – with some delightful strokeplay."

"I was up at the Pavilion End and Garry was back for his second spell bowling his spinners," says Lewis. "Malcolm was out to the first delivery of the over, I played a couple of dot balls and then I remember giving Garry some of his own medicine. I didn't think 'Oh… I'm going to hit him for six!' but the ball was slightly on leg and I put it just behind square over the short boundary – where Garry had smashed Malcolm for his first six when batting at the sea end. I didn't think I was our answer to Garry Sobers but I did hit a couple of fours off the next two balls to round off the over."

Fourteen runs off one over from the world's greatest all-rounder wasn't a bad start – and it proved the bedrock of an important innings as Lewis and Walker gradually edged Glamorgan to safety with a stand of 73 in 42 minutes.

"I was a tailender who considered himself a batsman – as we all did," recalls Lewis. "I always wanted to bat as well as bowl. For one of those two fours, I think Garry bowled me a quick one. I saw it coming and had a go at it. A little later, he bowled his chinaman and I read it: I could see it through the air and the way it was turning from off to leg. I played forward and left it – and Peter Walker fell about laughing at the other end, he was collapsed in a heap! He thought I'd mis-read it, that it was pure luck I wasn't out, but that was his sense of humour."

With Glamorgan's score at 237, Lewis lifted Bob White high over the boundary for his second six to avoid the follow-on – passing his previous best score of 32 in the process – before eventually being run out for 38 with the score at 252.

"From what I can remember," he says, "it was just one of those mix-ups but despite that, it was a big thrill for me to hit my top score in that match. I took my batting seriously and that was the highlight of my career at the crease as we saved the follow-on."

In a match full of sixes, Walker's unbeaten innings of 104 didn't contain a single one. He batted, as *Wisden* recorded, "steadily for his second century of the season in two hours, forty minutes." The 10th hundred of his career took 157 minutes, included 14 fours and, as Pat Gibson, writing in *The Nottingham Guardian Journal*, explained, "saved some semblance of Welsh pride after the pounding it had taken on Saturday."

"I recall being very pleased that I had faced and survived Garry in all three of his bowling guises – fast-medium, slow left-arm orthodox leg-spin and alternative wrist-spin – because I could mainly read what he was trying to do from his hand action at release," recalls Walker. "When he tried his wrist-spin from the Mumbles Road End, I could see the difference between his chinaman – an off-break to a right-handed batsman – and his googly, which looked like an off-break but in fact spun the other way! At one stage, Garry grinned down the wicket and said, 'hey man...you can pick it!' and soon went back to bowling his quicker variety."

At 32, Walker was one of the more experienced members of the Glamorgan team. He had made his debut against Leicestershire in 1956 when he scored a duck and two but took the first of 697 first class catches in a 16 year career during which he became the county's greatest ever close fielder – equally adept on both sides of the wicket. Tall and agile, Walker earned himself the nickname of 'Flypaper

Fingers' as he fielded fearlessly in a variety of positions – mainly at short square leg or leg-slip but also moving over into the slips to follows likely edges when needed. Having switched from medium-paced swing bowling to orthodox left-arm spin, he developed into a fine all-rounder and played three times for England against South Africa in 1960 – scoring 128 runs in four innings, holding on to five catches and bowling 13 overs without taking a wicket. Along with the other England spinners, Ray Illingworth and Bob Barber, Walker was hardly needed as Fred Trueman, Brian Statham and Middlesex's Alan Moss comprehensively destroyed South Africa in the first three Tests. With the series wrapped up, the selectors decided to experiment in the two remaining Tests and, despite achieving what was arguably the finest treble in the history of first-class cricket – 1,347 runs, 101 wickets and 73 catches – in the next season, Walker was never given another chance at international level.

One of Walker's other personal highlights of the 1968 season had come during the match against Hampshire at Cardiff. It was the first championship game to be played on a Sunday in Wales and, according to *Wisden,* turned out to be a "bit hit" with a crowd of 5,000, producing gate receipts of £500. Replying to Hampshire's first innings total of 145, Majid Khan (91) and Tony Lewis (53) helped give Glamorgan a 68-run lead and after Tony Cordle had taken four for 24, Walker weighed in with three wickets in five balls to finish with five for nine from nearly four overs as Glamorgan won by an innings.

Walker then took a crucial wicket in the defeat of Australia at St Helen's in August. Just as Paul Sheahan looked set to win the match for the tourists, he was caught and bowled by the all-rounder. "I sent down a genuine long hop," he recalls, "and he whacked it back right off the middle of the bat and I managed to hang on to a fierce return straight drive. It was a pretty handy catch but a disgraceful ball to get a bloke out for 137."

After scoring 96 and taking five for 66 as Glamorgan beat Somerset at Taunton, Walker exerted little influence with bat or ball in the 100-run defeat by Derbyshire which ended Glamorgan's hopes of wining the championship. As he made his way down to Swansea for the game against Nottinghamshire, he knew there would be a sizeable Bank Holiday crowd at St Helen's — because of one man.

"In those days, if Garry played he attracted a decent-sized crowd because he was the world's greatest ever player — in anybody's reckoning," says Walker. "The man was unique, the sort of animal who was always going to win you a game. When you were up against a team which included him, you were playing against 13 men — he was worth at least two extra men because he wasn't your bog-standard all-rounder. He was a wonderful bowler of several varieties, an absolutely world-class batsman and a fantastic catcher but he wasn't the world's greatest captain. It doesn't automatically follow that the best player is the best captain. I thought it was a good and brave move by Sobers and Nottinghamshire for him to join them in 1968. It showed that they weren't satisfied to finish down the bottom all the time so they just signed the best player the game had ever seen. Money would have been the big lure for Garry but he was also the sort of bloke who revelled in that type of situation: he always played at his best when the going was toughest."

Walker had found the going quite tough as he and his Glamorgan team-mates struggled to contain the Nottinghamshire batsmen — especially when their skipper raced to 40 before launching his savage assault on Malcolm Nash. In tandem with Shepherd earlier in the innings, Walker had managed to slow down the run rate but he came in for some stick later on as 51 runs — more than half those he conceded — were hit off his last 12 overs. He was replaced by Shepherd who Sobers hit for nine runs in the last over before Nash bowled his famous one.

It took 35 seconds for the ball to be returned to Nash

after Sobers had smashed him out of the ground for the first six. The part-time spinner picked it up, examined it, spun it in his hands, surveyed the field for a second and licked his fingers as he moved forward. Eddie Phillipson and the close fielders went through their crouching ritual again, John Parkin edged down the wicket and Sobers tapped his bat in the crease 10 times before unleashing his second hammer blow.

"My mind-set didn't change even though I had been hit for six," says Nash. "You might say that's not a too clever thought process but it has always registered in my mind that unless you bowl at the wicket, you're not going to get anybody out. The straighter you bowl, the more batsmen have to play and the more chances they have of making mistakes. I've always focused on that."

"I believe that Malcolm thought the first six seemed to be a mis-hit so he tried putting it there again," says Sobers. "Instead of bowling the first ball at middle and leg, he drifted it a little bit over the off stump and I hit him over mid-on. Because the second ball was aimed more at the leg stump, I hit it a little bit squarer."

The ball flew over the heads of Alan Rees and Brian Lewis at mid-wicket, over a wall and out of the ground. As spectators started to search for it, the ball was thrown back by someone on the other side of the wall. Up in the commentary box, Wilf Wooller, like the crowd, was starting to warm up:

"That's another one! Goodness gracious me! That's peppered the top – you can see the chap climbing up there to have a look over the wall. That peppered another hotel the other side of St Helen's…a magnificent shot, picked it on the up. Glamorgan could do with a few fielders stuck on the top of that wall over there – some seven footers."

"I can remember Malcolm talking to himself during the over," recalls Parkin, "and saying things like 'Where do I bowl the next one? Do I put it up there or bowl it quicker?' He didn't say it after every ball – just once or twice."

"There was no change in my approach when the second ball went over mid-wicket," recalls Nash. "The object of the exercise for me as a slow bowler was to get Garry to hit the ball in the air. Later on in that over, my approach was justified."

"I thought I was going to catch the first two sixes," recalls Brian Lewis. "From the way that Garry played the shots, I thought to myself 'I'm in with a shout here!' but they didn't come down, they just kept going."

"When the over started to take shape, I just felt very glad that it wasn't happening to me," admits Walker. "There wasn't much that anyone could do about it. Malcolm had the ball, he had to let it go and he was a very capable bowler."

But having switched from seam to spin, Nash's new line in bowling was now on the line. Under-rehearsed, the Underwood lookalike was under fire. Sobers had hit 52 runs in 32 minutes, 12 of them from the first two balls of the over. Impersonation may be the sincerest form of flattery but, in this case, it was threatening to become the most expensive too. Superman needed to act – and act fast.

THE THIRD BALL

As Majid Jahangir Khan stood idly in the slips watching Garry Sobers score his six sixes, he *almost* knew how the Nottinghamshire captain was feeling — almost but not quite.

Just over a year earlier, on the same cricket square in St Helen's, Majid had narrowly failed to become The History Man himself — by dint of a dot ball fired wide down the leg side in response to his hitting the first delivery of the over for six.

Both batsmen were interested in quick runs but there the similarity ended. While Sobers was oblivious to records, Majid was obsessed with one in particular. Scoring the fastest century of the season meant nothing to the West Indian but absolutely everything to the Pakistani tourist as he hammered Glamorgan off-spinner Roger Davis for five sixes in a single over. With overseas players being allowed into the English game in 1968, Sobers had been happy to help out struggling Nottinghamshire but Majid was aiming higher. He hoped he could use his quick-fire hundred to land a top job in English county cricket. It was a means to an end: an historic place in the record books would produce a coveted place in a successful team.

"I always wanted to play in England because county cricket was different to the first-class game in Pakistan," says Majid. "Our game was based on a knock-out system of eight teams so a side which went through to the final only played, at the most, three matches a season. It all depended on a first-innings lead. The two strongest teams were Lahore and Karachi and they used to bat for two days, put the other side in on the third day, bowl them out and that was the end of the game. The rest of the time we were playing club cricket — one-day games like the Sunday League in England – and I wanted to play first-class county cricket where it all mattered."

Having earmarked Glamorgan as his whipping boys rather than one of his preferences, Majid proceeded to achieve his first target by reaching his hundred in 61 minutes en route to making 147 in Pakistan's second innings. But his second ambition proved more problematic. As he smote their bowlers all around St Helen's, Majid had no intention of joining Glamorgan; in fact, they were barely on his radar. From researching the records, he knew that, apart from a championship win in 1948 and a couple of promising seasons in the first half of the 1960s, they had spent most of their first-class existence in the bottom half of the table. He was grateful for their help in promoting his career but they were the last side he had thought about signing for. But he had reckoned without the wily Wilf Wooller, the former Glamorgan captain and their then secretary.

"After my innings at Swansea, I thought there would be a few offers but none came – except the one from Glamorgan!" recalls Majid. "It seems that Wilf, who'd been a contemporary of my father, Jahangir's, at Cambridge University before the Second World War, had whispered the word that I was going to be signing for Glamorgan so he stamped out all the other counties. Nobody else asked for my services so I came to Wales – I had no choice."

It turned out to be one of the best moves, both professional and personal, that Majid ever made. As Glamorgan entered a golden era with three top-three championship finishes between 1968 and 1970, the graceful and dashing import added an edge of elegant élan to the county's batting line-up – especially during the championship-winning season of 1969. Like Sobers, Majid was not only a world-class batsman; he brought out the best in his team-mates. Encouraged by his example, to a man, they scaled new heights. His confidence, born of youth because he was only

21 when he joined under-performing Glamorgan, permeated through the dressing room.

"The big leap from the bottom of the table to the top came in 1968," recalls skipper Tony Lewis, "by which time I had seen proof that one brilliant individual can lift the play of others. Majid showed us how talented he was against any opposition and how unselfish a great cricketer can be. It used to be so easy to tramp round the first-class circuit in comfortable mediocrity. Glamorgan found inspiration and courage in Majid. He transformed the county in his day because everyone else played to the limits of their talent, too."

"A batting genius, if ever I saw one," is Peter Walker's pithy assessment of the magical Majid.

"I enjoyed my time with Glamorgan because the atmosphere was very relaxed, much more friendly than I thought it would be," says Majid who, after retiring from cricket in the 1980s, pursued a career in broadcasting and cricket administration. "My colleagues were a very happy bunch, they had a good sense of humour and because of Glamorgan's tradition of not being a very influential county and not always being in the top half of the championship table, they were much more relaxed in that they knew their shortcomings and their strengths. They were good players who had confidence in their ability. Don Shepherd, Alan Jones, Peter Walker and Tony Lewis had played together over the years and they understood each other very well. It was a very nice atmosphere so I started to enjoy playing with the team. Then we also became a winning side and when you are winning, the atmosphere becomes even better."

At times, Majid's team-mates considered him diffident, even disinterested and it took him a while to bed in. Although he top scored with 31 on a rain-affected Sophia Gardens wicket in his first championship match against Leicestershire in Cardiff, Majid, by his own admission, had a patchy debut season. There were decent scores against

Hampshire (91), Sussex (101), Northampton (72 not out) and he hit 55 when the Australians were beaten at St Helen's but too often he failed to turn promising starts into big innings. It all came to a head when Glamorgan played Derbyshire in the middle of August when Majid opened with Roger Davis and was bowled by Ian Buxton for 28 with the score at 48 for two.

"I was having a bad spell at that time and in a patch like that, you play atrocious shots," he recalls. "It was very cold and windy at Derby that day and the fire hardly worked in the dressing room. When I came back to the pavilion, I was feeling very despondent and disgusted with myself. I felt that as a professional overseas player, I wasn't doing the basic job properly – I wasn't doing what was required of me. So I found the groundsman and asked him if he had a saw. He was a bit puzzled but went off to find one. When he brought it back, I cut my bat in half. I was getting a bit fed up with it because I hadn't made many runs lately. Obviously, I came up with the lame excuse that it was the bat's fault rather than the man behind the bat. 1968 hadn't been a great first season in England for me and I took out my anger and frustration on that bat. I suddenly became a carpenter for about five minutes and left the two halves in the dressing room but I didn't do any better with its replacement – scoring only 12 in the second innings."

But from then on, Majid began to show his true form as Glamorgan maintained their title challenge. He hit 85 against Surrey, a highest score of the season of 123 and 61 against Somerset, 80 in the defeat by Derby just before the Nottinghamshire game at Swansea and he ended the season with a championship average of 30.68. As an occasional bowler, he took six wickets and held 35 catches as he became a fully paid-up member of Glamorgan's outstanding club of close fielders.

Majid's recollections of cricket's most famous over are

not the most vivid. From his position alongside wicket-keeper Eifion Jones, he recalls Nottinghamshire's big opening partnership and Nash's big moment when he was finally given the chance to try out his spinners. If at first you don't succeed, try, try again...

"When I joined Glamorgan in 1968," says Majid, "we held the pre-season nets at the indoor school at Neath. I always remember that after bowling his fast-medium pace, Malcolm would turn to his slower stuff and after every ball which he'd bowled reasonably well, he would turn around and look very expectantly at Tony Lewis as if to say 'here I am, I can bowl spinners.' I didn't face them in the nets – he'd bowl them to the lower-order batsmen – and on that partic-ular day against Nottinghamshire, after we had been thrashed all over the place by their openers, Tony was looking around for bowlers. I remember seeing Malcolm, bursting with enthusiasm, so Tony let him try his hand at spinners."

Majid's abiding memory of the six sixes is not the over itself but part of the fallout from it and, in particular, a con-versation Nash would continue to have with their team-mate, Don Shepherd, one of the most parsimonious bowlers to have played county cricket.

"Once the last six went out of the ground," says Majid, "Don didn't stop shaking his head. After the close of play of any later match, he would always bring up the subject over a drink by asking Malcolm a question: 'How did you allow him to hit you for six sixes? I can't understand. You could have bowled him a ball down the leg-side or a wide outside the off stump or a faster one. I still can't understand how you got hit for six sixes!'"

In the immediate aftermath of the history-making innings, Majid did much to stabilise an unsteady ship after Roger Davis was dismissed for a duck when Glamorgan replied to Nottinghamshire's total of 394 for five declared. He can't remember much about his time at the crease but according to *The Observer's* correspondent, he played "with skill against a varied attack" in helping to take the score to 78 before holing out for 41. Majid made only four in Glamorgan's second innings but did pick up a smart catch when Nottinghamshire batted again. A report in the *South Wales Echo* revealed that Mike Smedley had snicked Tony Cordle low to slip "where Majid plucked a one-handed catch with deceptive ease."

The words, "deceptive ease", could just as well have been applied to the way in which Don Shepherd bowled. Like Majid's batting and fielding, Shep made it all look ridiculously easy, like a stroll in the park. According to Tony Lewis in his foreword to Douglas Miller's *Born to Bowl: The Life and Times of Don Shepherd*, Shep was so good because "he settled upon a style, a speed and an action that came naturally out of his body…Don Shepherd's eventual run-up and delivery came perfectly from within: never strained, never too fast and certainly not too slow, but just right. It was if someone had set a metronome ticking and left it running for over twenty years and for over two thousand wickets."

Shepherd had made his first-class debut in 1950 against Surrey at The Oval as a seamer but five years later he switched styles to become a medium-pace off-spinner and developed into one of the finest bowlers never to have played for England. His country's loss was his county's gain as, season after season, Shepherd's combination of stamina, consistency, control and accuracy brought him a staggering number of wickets on either slow turners or plumb batsmen's pitches. He had already been awarded a benefit by Glamorgan and in the brochure for his 1968 testimonial season, John Arlott wrote that "in certain, and frequent, conditions, he is the most effective bowler in modern county cricket."

1968 had always promised to be an important year for Shepherd. As well as the testimonial, a just reward for his 21 years of loyal service to the county, the Australians were touring again. Shep sensed something might be in the air when he ended the prologue to his testimonial brochure on this nationalistic and prophetically optimistic note:

"We feel that we carry the responsibility of first-class cricket in Wales each game we play. When things go wrong, we are as disappointed as the spectator. Therefore I hope that we can rise above our form of the last two seasons and make this Australian summer one to be remembered."

The fact that almost everything went right when the tourists arrived at St Helen's a month before the Nottinghamshire match was due, in no small measure, to Shepherd. With skipper Tony Lewis forced out of the game through illness, Shep took over the reins and Glamorgan triumphed against the Australians again – the first time the tourists had been beaten by a county side on consecutive visits to Britain. He had been instrumental in the 36-run win at Swansea four years earlier by finishing with the remarkable bowling analysis of 52-29-71-5, having already taken four for 22 from 17 overs in the first innings, but this time it was Shep's shrewd captaincy which thwarted the tourists.

"It was a completely different game of cricket to 1964 on a very good track," he recalls. "I enjoyed being in charge because I had a theory that a bowling captain has some advantages over a batting captain – bowlers think more about field placings and things like that. But I've got to say that it's the easy way to do it because an acting captain doesn't have to go and deal with committees and team selection. It was vital to win the toss against Australia and it was a good surface but you would have expected, knowing the history of St Helen's, a bit of help for the spinners on the last day. In fact, it did turn a little bit but it remained basically a very good pitch and we got lots of runs. I remember Alan Jones scored 99, Majid and Bryan and Roger Davis made a few and Nashy picked up some wickets. I had two slogs and got 10 and 14 as last man in.

"Australia wanted 365 on the last day and it sounds a lot but it was a full day's cricket because we used to bowl 20 overs an hour in those days. Although Australia always liked going for a win, there would have come a time when they knew they couldn't win and would then try to save the match. Because I'd been brought up in our family's village shop in Parkmill in Gower, I could work out the runs and the overs instantly and I wanted the Australians to keep going. I didn't want them to shut up shop so they had to have a sniff of it all the time. They kept going and I think it was great credit to them that they played the game in that way – in the right spirit. Brian Lewis bowled non-stop for 32 overs, I had five fewer and I used myself as a brake on scoring as much as trying to get people out. It was very special as I was captain and we got this wonderful response from the team again. To beat the Australians twice in four years was magnificent."

As he watched Nottinghamshire build their substantial first-innings total, Shepherd wasn't at all surprised by the number of sixes being scored in the match. He was well aware of the reputation St Helen's had gained for being a big-hitters' paradise because, as a no-nonsense tailender, he had helped to create it through a series of spectacular knocks. One 15-minute innings against the Australians in 1961, when he equalled a word record by hitting 51 with just 11 scoring shots, included three sixes each off Richie Benaud and Lindsay Kline.

Shepherd himself had conceded three sixes by the time he had bowled the last of his 25 wicketless overs against Nottinghamshire and a single to Sobers off his final delivery had, unwittingly, set up the famous assault. He may have ribbed Nash mercilessly about being hit for six sixes but he was sympathetic to his plight. As the county's finest ever bowler, Shepherd knew a thing or two about dealing with the best cricketers in the world – especially one who was looking for a quick declaration on a superb batting track. While some people have claimed that Nash was simply bowling his 'Sunday League stuff' to Sobers, Shep is more than happy to defend the part-time spinner.

"Although Malcolm was experimenting," he recalls, "he was bowling properly. It wasn't foolish stuff – wide or anything like that. He was trying to get the ball to turn back in to Garry. He probably thought that if he could get him out by bowling left-arm spin rather than his normal seam-up that would be a great achievement."

Both Ossie Wheatley and Tony Lewis have publicly acknowledged the debt they owe Shepherd for the advice he gave them during their spells as captain of Glamorgan. He was their right-hand man whose experience proved invaluable in turning around the county's fortunes. As a keen student of the game, Shep was forever analysing his opponents, constantly looking for ways of taking their wicket. He was, says Lewis, "full of consummate understanding of what a different length is to different batsmen…it would all be in there, a spool ready to run as soon as he saw someone walking to the crease." Like most bowlers, Shep's knowledge was put to the test when the new batsman was Garry Sobers.

"A lot of off-spinners go round the wicket to left-handers but I had a theory about bowling over the wicket," he says. "I felt that if I was accurate enough when bowling at Garry, if I could pitch the ball on leg stump or within an inch or two, then he wasn't the sort of bloke to play the sweep shot. I don't remember him playing many. I knew he was always going to get runs but I felt that I could at least keep him in some sort of check by bowling a very tight leg-side line. That's what I always did. How successful I was I don't know…but I did manage to bowl him in the second innings of the six sixes game – albeit for 72 runs."

In fact, Shepherd had almost picked up the most prized wicket in English cricket when he made a ball leave the bat at the start of the Nottinghamshire captain's second innings but

Sobers, on four, escaped with an edge to the boundary. Shep's perseverance paid off when, after being hit for a flurry of fours, he induced Sobers to chop a ball on to his stumps. In the *Nottinghamshire Evening Post*, Pat Gibson reported that "Shepherd got his reward for an impressive piece of bowling against the great West Indian."

After Sobers and John Parkin had crossed for a single at the end of Shepherd's final over in Nottinghamshire's first innings, the veteran spinner made his way from the stumps at the Mumbles Road End down to short third man and watched Malcolm Nash's first two deliveries go sailing over the leg-side boundary. After the second six, the ball was returned from the other side of a wall within seconds and as it bounced back into the field of play, Brian Lewis went to pick it up. But Nash himself had come to the edge of the square to collect it. He walked back to the start of his run-up, examining and rubbing the ball all the while, but instead of stopping, broke straight into his stride.

"To me," says Nash, "Garry was the best player in the world, the greatest player that I played against and I wanted to get him out. And the only way to do that was by attacking him – and that's exactly what I did."

Nash ran in past umpire Eddie Phillipson and the expectant Nottinghamshire batsman, John Parkin, and Sobers tapped his bat on the ground another 10 times before executing his third shot.

"Malcolm was one of those players who always tried and my wicket was very important to him," recalls Sobers. "With his third delivery, he went a little bit wider and I really hit this one. The straight boundaries weren't very big, I really got hold of it and the ball went right up over long-off and into the crowd."

The power of the superbly timed drive forced Sobers to lift his right foot off the ground and Parkin, Nash and Phillipson had to turn and crane their necks to follow the flight of the ball as it disappeared high over Roger Davis at long-off before landing in the members' enclosure in front of the pavilion. Some spectators rose to their feet to applaud Sobers; a man clutching a pint of beer in each hand carefully negotiated a flight of concrete steps back to his seat and a thirsty friend. The supporter who caught the ball about five rows from the top of the enclosure immediately threw it down towards the square but it didn't clear the wall at the bottom so another spectator bent down and flicked it up to Davis who then returned it to Nash.

"As the over went on," says Shepherd, "it was quite obvious that six sixes were on and Garry kept on going. If it had been me, I would probably have changed sooner in the over. I would have tried something else when I could see what was happening but Malcolm persevered because he never thought he couldn't get somebody out."

"All the while, I was just thinking that Garry was going for quick runs," admits Parkin, "but, looking back, I realise I should have known more about what was happening in terms of him going for six sixes. The whole thing went above my head; I wasn't counting the sixes and making the connection. I was still looking to get on strike but there was no chance – Garry wasn't even looking at me for a run."

"When the first half of the over was being bowled," recalls Graham Frost, Nottinghamshire's rookie batsman, "I was walking from the Mumbles Road End, right past the rugby stand and across the open boundary to the members' enclosure. I wasn't too interested in the first two or three balls but, all of a sudden, everybody was getting excited so I made a dash back up to the steps to the pavilion where I watched the rest of the over."

"That's another one … up in the enclosure!" cried Wilf Wooller as the excitement levels started to rise in the BBC Wales commentary box. "The last person we saw hit like this was Majid Jahangir in that wonderful knock against

Glamorgan a year ago."

The Pakistani master craftsman was now standing alone in the safety of the slips – relieved that an earlier back injury meant he would never be anything more than an occasional bowler. Forty summers later, he refuses to criticise the team's experimental spinner.

"Malcolm might have bowled a ball that was not hittable, one that Garry couldn't have hit out of the ground or over the boundary," maintains Majid, "so his attitude – to try and get Garry out – was the right one: he wanted his wicket desperately. What would I have done? It's a very difficult question to answer."

As the ball was returned to him, Malcolm Nash was facing a very similar dilemma: what should he do now? A different approach had been tried by pitching the ball on the off-side but it had produced the same result. At the halfway point of the over, there had been no half measures from Sobers. Three balls, 18 runs. Help!

THE FOURTH BALL

Tony Lewis had seen enough. It was time for action. Having given Glamorgan's experimental spinner his head, it had become his responsibility, as captain, to try to help him keep it. The first three balls of Malcom Nash's 15th over of spin had been hit for six and damage limitation was the name of the game. Not so much because of the sizeable score being quickly compiled – it had now reached 376 – as the state of the battered bowler. Like a beaten boxer, Nash was reeling on the ropes, Sobers was winning The Battle of the Supermen hands down and Lewis realised that although he couldn't throw in the towel, he needed to lob Nash some sort of lifeline. As the ball was returned from in front of the members' enclosure by Roger Davis, the captain wandered over from his position at mid-off to have a quiet word.

"I wanted to give Malcolm the chance to end the experiment and get back to his seam and swing bowling," Lewis recalls. "I tried to persuade him to bowl seamers for the last three balls.

"'Look after yourself now,' I said.

"'What do you mean?'

"'Well you've just gone for three sixes so if you want to go over the wicket with your usual seam-up stuff and get them as near to the blockhole as you can, then that's fine by me.'

"I can't remember his precise words but Malcolm said something to the effect of 'Leave it with me – I'm in control. Don't worry. I'll get him any minute now.' That was typical Malcolm – he was always very confident but he had entered the dangerous area where pride moves in, but on rubber legs. It was as if he were fighting Muhammad Ali and refusing a stool after being knocked down three times in the last round."

"I must admit," says Nash, "that I don't recall that conversation about reverting to seam-up. It's possible that Tony came up and gave me some encouragement after the third ball but I can't be sure. My recollection is more of me looking at Tony and him just smiling back at me and saying 'carry on bowling'. In retrospect, I might well have been better to go back to my normal style but I felt the only way to get Garry out was to bowl straight – which is what I tried to do."

At this time, Lewis, a regular in the Glamorgan side since 1960, was approaching the end of his second season as captain. He had succeeded Ossie Wheatley in 1967 after scoring more than 2,000 runs during the previous summer through his skilful and graceful batting. His first year in charge had been anything but easy: he averaged only 19 in the championship as the county again finished 14th in the table and won only three games. But during the winter of 1967-68, Lewis toured Pakistan with a Commonwealth team where he learned much from the captaincy of the Australian, Richie Benaud.

"He never fussed over players," recalls Lewis. "Either they did well or they didn't. He would advise but only when asked and he wouldn't waste words. It was if he saw random thinking and spoken words as energy leaving the body. On or off the field, he thought everything through and, once prepared, was positive and bold. 'Be two overs ahead of play' was his life's mantra – 'and be lucky.' It was a rewarding experience to play under his captaincy, no detail too small for his attention, and all directed at attack. The Benaud coat of arms might bear the motto 'domination by preparation'."

Lewis returned from Pakistan refreshed, reinvigorated and raring to go, armed with an adventurous blueprint for success. A relentless quest for batting points and a positive approach to declarations would prove crucial weapons in Glamorgan's armoury. With the arrival of Majid Khan from Pakistan and the emergence of young players such as Nash, Brian Lewis and Roger Davis, Lewis made astute use of the experience of Peter Walker, Ossie Wheatley, Alan Jones and Don Shepherd to mould together a team which mounted a serious, if ultimately unsuccessful challenge for the championship. His average barely rose to just over 22, his highest score of 112 was made against Cambridge University as he narrowly failed to reach 1,000 championship runs, but he managed to engineer four victories through decisive declarations.

But on August Bank Holiday Saturday 1968 at St Helen's, Lewis was on the receiving end. Having lost the toss and thus the opportunity to bat first, he was waiting for Sobers to declare as the Nottinghamshire total headed towards 400. It was merely a matter of time and there was little he could do but wait for the inevitable. During the innings, Lewis had used seven bowlers with Nash and his Underwood-style spinners, ironically, proving the most successful. When the West Indian captain came to the crease, his opposite number knew what to expect.

"Garry had always played with great power and style," he says. "I think he had come in to speed things up and he batted normally for a while. But then I think he thought 'this is ridiculous, we're 30 short, let's give it a whack and we might get 15.' He was good enough to decide that he was going to hit the next ball for six – and maybe the next one and maybe the next one.

"I ought to point out that this particular over was nothing to do with field placing. I take no blame for it at all. We weren't into the business of major tactics at that stage. We were on the hind hoof and it didn't matter where we fielded – unless it was on either King Edward's Road or St Helen's Avenue. I was at mid-off – you can see me on the BBC Wales footage of the over – but most people were on the boundary. Once we'd picked up Gary's intentions, there was no point in crowding him."

Opening batsman Alan Jones was fielding at square leg, not

far from the scoreboard on the Gorse Lane side of the ground. As the total kept rising, the man who would become the county's record scorer with more than 40,000 runs in all forms of the game, was looking forward to getting to work on such a placid pitch but he was also keeping half an eye on the clock. Once Sobers declared, Jones and Roger Davis would have the tricky task of batting for an hour before stumps and he was starting to prepare himself for what he hoped would be a long innings. Unlike some of his team-mates, Jones had first-hand experience of playing against the West Indian captain. After a successful West Indies tour to Australia in 1960-61, Sobers signed for South Australia for three seasons. In the middle one, 1962-63, he became the first player ever to achieve the double of 1,000 runs and 50 wickets in Australian first-class cricket and he repeated the feat the following season. By this time, Jones had been signed by Western Australia for whom he would play eight Sheffield Shield matches during the 1963-64 season – including a four-day match which began on New Year's Day 1964 at the WACA, the headquarters of the Western Australia Cricket Association in Perth.

"We batted first and made 200 with me top scoring with 37," Jones recalls. "South Australia were 38 for one in reply at the end of the first day's play. When the players had a drink in the dressing rooms afterwards, Garry, who was a big gambler, said he was going over to the Gloucester Park horse-trotting course across the road. Some of our team went over there too but we never saw him. As I came back from the nets the next day, Garry was going towards them. Normally, he never had a net because he was involved so much in the game with his batting, bowling and fielding.

"'How did you get on last night?' I asked.

"'Oh…terrible,' replied Garry. 'I lost £150.'

"The Australian currency is dollars but Garry's contract with South Australia was in pounds and back in 1964, £150 was a lot of money – in any currency. 'But,' Garry said, 'I'm going to make it back today.'

"At the time, I had no idea what he meant but he had his net and came out to bat at 182 for five. Garry scored 195 – as they made 497 all out. That night, I asked him to explain the previous night's comment.

"'South Australia pay me a pound for every run I score over 50 in any Sheffield Shield innings,' Garry said. 'It's in my contract.'

"So he'd virtually made it back. For the record, we scored 342 in our second innings – I made 51 – and they won by nine wickets."

Sobers wasn't playing when the efficient and reliable Jones scored an unbeaten 161 against the West Indies at St Helen's in 1966. Two years later, Glamorgan's batting equivalent of Don Shepherd was a third of the way through a 23-year career in which he never failed to score 1,000 runs per season. John Arlott's appreciation in *Wisden Cricket Monthly* sums up the way Jones went out the business of batting:

"Fundamentally correct and determined, he created the left-hander's stock impression of heavy-handedness. In addition to all the shifts and nudges of the opening batsman against the new ball, he played with controlled power though the arc between cover point and mid-on. At need, too, he could push the scoring rate along by resource rather than slogging."

1968 was proving to be a particularly profitable season for Jones who would accumulate more than 1,700 runs in all competitions – including the fourth 99 of his career when the Australian tourists arrived at St Helens earlier that August. After opening with Roger Davis, he scored nearly half of Glamorgan's first innings total of 224 before his anti-climactic demise:

"It was very frustrating," he recalls, "but, to be honest, it was a bad shot. I'd played very well up until then but, as my career record shows, I seemed to get a little bit nervous in the 90s. It was a good wicket, it wasn't really turning and their off-spinner, Ashley Mallett, came on to bowl. Neil Hawke was three quarters of the way back to the boundary at long-on and I could have played the ball into the covers and just looked for the single. Instead, I went down the wicket and tried to hit him over the top and, as Neil went backwards, he caught me. It would have been a big plus to have got a hundred against the Australians but we won which was the main thing."

Ten day later, Jones made an unbeaten 95 to help Glamorgan beat Lancashire in Cardiff which had skipper Tony Lewis waxing lyrical in his round-up of the season in the club's members' newsletter the following December:

"Certainly, Alan Jones' superb consistency played a vital part and who of those who endured the black wintry conditions at Sophia Gardens will ever forget his innings against Lancashire? One of the best in the club's history."

Praise indeed and it was also turning out to be a very hot summer for Alan's younger brother, Eifion – from his position behind the stumps and in front of them too. Six years Alan's junior, he had just taken over the wicket-keeper's gloves from David Evans having originally joined Glamorgan as a middle-order batsman. Under the guidance of coach Phil Clift, Jones quickly developed the catching skills he had effectively employed in the slips.

"Eifion came to us as a batsman," recalls Clift. "We were short of a wicket-keeper in the second team and I'd noticed he was pretty good with his hands – he'd field in the slips and he'd catch most things.

"'Have you ever kept?' I asked him one day.

"'No,' he said. Eifion was a man of very few words.

"'Would you like to have a go?'

"'All right.'

"'Right, we'll get you some gloves and see what you think of it.'

"And he was a natural!"

After his brother's important opening knock against the Australians, Eifion Jones had taken two catches off Malcolm Nash in the tourists' first innings and as they threatened to overhaul the winning target through Bob Cowper and Paul Sheahan, he held on to a skier off Brian Lewis to dismiss Cowper for 42. He finished the season with 65 victims, second only to Nottinghamshire's Deryck Murray.

Don Shepherd remembers Jones as "a tough little batsman and a fine keeper in all conditions, standing up or standing back" – even though Jones didn't always agree with Shepherd's request for him to stand back, especially on slow wickets.

During the 1968 season, he responded superbly to a shortage of middle-order runs by scoring more than any post-war Glamorgan keeper in any one summer. His total in all competitions of 825 included a club record unbeaten 146 against Sussex at Hove in June during an unbroken third-wicket partnership of 230 with his brother. Forty years later, his innings still stands as the highest score ever made by a Glamorgan gloveman.

Although he would later make 29 out of a fifth-wicket partnership of 59 with Peter Walker to help Glamorgan avoid the follow-on, Jones had endured a fruitless day during Nottinghamshire's first innings. There had been no stumpings or catches with out-fielders responsible for four of the five dismissals and Nash bowling Murray for the other. When Sobers arrived at the crease, the Jones boys, one at very close range, could only stand and admire the brilliance of the West Indian's shots.

"Although everyone talks about that over," says Alan Jones, "as soon as Garry came in that day, he just middled everything. To be honest, some of his shots through the covers on the floor were far better than the six sixes. He hit some cracking shots but then he just cut loose when he started looking for a declaration. It looked to me that he was going to bat for half an hour, or just over, so he could put us in for 45 minutes or maybe an hour later that evening.

"When the first six went, I just thought it was another typical Sobers shot over the top. Nobody in their wildest dreams would have thought that he'd go on to hit another five. It never entered anybody's mind. But then he hit the second and then the third."

Having given Nash a mini-pep talk, Tony Lewis returned to mid-off. As he saw it, he had done his duty to his bowler by suggesting that his spinners be replaced by his more familiar seamers. It was now up to Superman. Lewis could do no more. As Sobers began to prepare for the fourth ball, Eifion Jones, crouched to the left of the stumps with hands on hips, looked towards the deep square leg boundary – almost as if he'd had some premonition about the destination of the next delivery. 'Watch out brother,' he seemed to be suggesting, 'this one's coming your way!'

As the wicket-keeper dropped to his haunches, John Parkin and Eddie Phillipson waited. Perhaps understandably, Nash wasn't approaching the crease with quite as much enthusiasm and his leading right arm was discernibly less upright in his delivery stride. This time, there were eight taps of the bat while Sobers waited, as *Wisden* recorded, "crouched like a black panther eager to pounce."

The special and very specific ball-by-ball account of the historic over in the 1969 *Glamorgan Yearbook* was less poetic and considerably more impolite, even brutal. Although it contained no personal by-line, the report bore all the hall-marks of having been written by the notoriously gruff Wilf Wooller. Having described the first three balls rather matter-of-factly, the anonymous author started to warm to his task:

"Nash came in to bowl his fourth ball under some strain. Three honest deliveries had produced the maximum 18 runs and although the wicket was easy paced and the boundaries not too distant, there was little more that a bowler could concede. Clearly undecided, as to where to pitch the next one, Nash pulled it down a little short and to the legs of Sobers, a delivery of quite questionable parentage. Sobers moved into the hooking position and hitting the ball on the up, pulled it high over square leg's head on to the stone terraces where it rattled like a cannon ball among the steps and spectators for a moment or two before trickling down into the dip."

"I bowled it within the target area," recalls Nash, "but you have to remember that Garry was a supreme player. My intentions didn't change at all. We still needed to get him out – if we did, we would bowl them out. There was encouragement from some of the players – although there weren't too many of them close to me at that stage! – and I think I can remember Don Shepherd shouting out 'keep it going!, keep going lad...you'll get him!'

"The fourth ball I hit just behind square," says Sobers. "I think Malcolm still figured that he would get me out."

"I was just backward of square on the leg-side and the ball went right over my head," recalls Alan Jones. "Someone in the crowd threw it back to me and I threw it back to Eifion. I was too far away from Malcolm to think about saying anything to him."

"I'd suggested to Malcolm that he should pitch it up and bowl his normal stuff but I'm not saying that if he had, then Garry wouldn't have hit those next three balls for six as well," says Tony Lewis. "It was terrific cricket, you could tell Garry had decided to do it and he wasn't worried about getting out. I didn't know what the world record was. I've never been one for records or scores. I'd never heard of anybody hitting six sixes and it never occurred to me at the time. I just thought 'this is the Sobers I know and love – fantastic!'"

"To get the balls into the air that day, they had to be levered," recalls the ex-Nottinghamshire batsman, Brian Bolus, who himself hit six sixes in the match. "They weren't bouncing waist high. Garry had to swing with everything he'd got and he had to wind himself up to do that."

"He's got the fourth one – it's up again!" shouted Wilf Wooller as the BBC Wales commentary box started to shake. "There it is, bouncing on the concrete – four sixes in four balls. We've had some very good hitting – a very good 140 by Bolus – but this makes him 64 – four sixes."

"They were fantastic shots," says Bolus' opening partner, Bob White. "After the fourth one, everybody on the ground was excited. There was no doubt about it – Garry would go for it and try to hit the whole lot for six."

"After the fourth ball," recalls John Parkin, "the crowd were getting worked up but I was still looking for the strike, thinking I was going to get down there."

As the ball was being returned to Nash, Eifion Jones struck up a short conversation with Sobers which tickled the great man's fancy. His famous gap-toothed grin spread briefly across his face and he settled back to the serious business of preparing for the fifth ball.

"Eifion doesn't talk about the over a lot," says Alan Jones. "To him, it was just another game, another day behind the wicket but, years ago, I remember asking him if he'd said anything to Garry. He told me that during that conversation, he jokingly challenged him: 'I bet you can't hit the last two balls for six!' Eifion didn't have much to do during the over but because of the way Garry played that day, he had to concentrate really hard. He couldn't afford to miss anything because if Garry had happened not to make contact with the ball or if he'd got a nick, Eifion would have had to stump him or catch him. But Garry never looked like missing the ball."

Malcolm Nash must have been the only person in St Helen's who was now hoping that his fifth ball would prove the exception to the rule. A miss would be much better than a mile, it would save his reputation. He was unlikely to know it but the world record for sixes scored from one over, not to mention the fastest hundred of the season, was starting to be talked about by some spectators.

Four down, two to go. Two-thirds of the over had produced 24 runs, Sobers had moved to 64 and Nottinghamshire were now on 382 for five. If only his teammates had given Nash a Superman costume as well as his nickname.

THE FIFTH BALL

During the six sixes over, Roger Davis had a couple of things on his mind. As he stood on the long-off boundary in front of the members' enclosure at St Helen's, he was thinking about the imminent Nottinghamshire declaration and also about a brick wall.

Up to a point, he could sympathise with Malcolm Nash. Davis had suffered a similar fate on the same ground a year earlier at the hands of his Glamorgan team-mate, Majid Khan, who was then playing for Pakistan. After his first delivery had been hit for six, Davis bowled the next ball down the leg-side and then saw the following four promptly dispatched over the boundary.

But this was different. Four sixes on the trot, Sobers in the swing of things and two balls to go. It would surely soon be over so Davis, like his opening partner, Alan Jones, had been clock-watching as the Nottinghamshire total continued to rise. He knew that every savage blow of Sobers' bat was bringing a declaration a step nearer and he was making preparations for what was likely to be an awkward hour's batting before close of play. He was also worried about that wall.

"When a declaration is due, you get your mind in the right state to bat four or five overs beforehand so I was thinking about getting up the steps into the pavilion and getting ready to open the batting in 10 minutes time," says Davis. "When the fourth six went over square leg, I started to come up with a plan in my head. I had played at St Helen's both for Glamorgan and Swansea and I knew that, not far behind the boundary at the Pavilion End, there was a small wall. It looked just that, a small wall, from the fielding side but on the other side, there was a seven or eight foot drop. During my career, I had seen fielders who, because they didn't know the ground all that well and hadn't noticed the wall, hadn't been able to stop after chasing a ball to the boundary and had gone over it. It could be pretty nasty so the one thing I decided in my mind on that day was that I wasn't going to go over that wall. If the ball was in the air and I was going backwards and lost my balance, I could break my neck. It was as serious as that. Garry had hit four sixes, he was going to declare soon so I thought it didn't matter and I was determined not to go over that wall."

Seconds later, Davis' decision to make his personal safety his priority would change the course of cricket history.

Davis had made his debut for Glamorgan as a middle-order batsman at the end of the 1964 season but didn't establish a permanent place in the first team until 1968 when he began to open regularly with Jones. Steady but not prolific, he caused a few eyebrows to be raised when he put Fred Trueman into the Bramall Lane floodlights for two sixes in an over as Glamorgan beat Yorkshire in Sheffield in early July and he scored a half-century against the Australian tourists. By the time of the Nottinghamshire game, Davis had accumulated nearly 800 championship runs, including a career-best 82 against Lancashire, and bowled a handful of largely wicketless overs. The key statistic though was his 31 catches – one more than Peter Walker, under whose personal tutelage he would develop into the county's top close fielder. Davis was a decent batsman, an occasional off-spinner and he prided himself on being a first-class fielder.

"I loved catching," he reflects. "If you're a good catcher, then you hope the ball comes to you. All the best catchers do and if you're a professional catcher like I was, you want the ball to come to you to show what you can do."

"I gradually handed over to Roger the mantle of short square leg, the fielding position which I'd made my own in the mid-1950s," recalls Walker. "He didn't let me down by continuing Glamorgan's reputation for producing a regular stream of high-quality, close-to-the wicket fielders. He was fit to be ranked with the best of them. Rather as I had looked for inspiration to Allan Watkins at the start of my career, Roger, both fearless and agile, regarded me as his mentor. We would spend hours practicing diving and catching exercises to improve our skills."

"I very rarely fielded in the outfield," says Davis. "I was either at short leg, in the slips or at gully. I can clearly remember being in the covers when Clive Lloyd was batting for Lancashire – it was like World War Three out there! I reckon I fielded at long-off two or three times in my whole career. I don't remember if I was out there just for Nashy's last over or if I'd been put there before then. When Garry hit the first two balls for six, I thought he was going for it and odds on, one would be coming my way – and it did. The third one went right over my head and into the enclosure. It was a fantastic shot."

Over on the other side of the sightscreen at long-on, Tony Cordle had watched in admiration as the first six flew high over his head and out of the ground. The 28-year-old Barbadian was in his fifth season with Glamorgan having arrived in Britain and initially worked for London Transport before coming to Cardiff to be with his brother and sister. He was employed as a shunter by British Rail before re-igniting an interest in the game and becoming a full-time cricketer for the next 17 years. He was to become an important member of Glamorgan's 1969 championship-winning side and had recorded a season-best seven for 43 as Hampshire were beaten by an innings at Cardiff in June 1968.

"Tony was a fast-medium bowler with the priceless gift of producing a wicket-taking ball in amongst some less-than-deadly deliveries," recalls Walker. "He was a hard-hitting tailend batsman and an enthusiastic, if somewhat, erratic fielder. He was also blessed with an infectious singing voice which lightened many a lengthy coach trip to away games. During weekend matches at Swansea, we would take visiting teams to a pub in Pontarddulais where we'd team up with members of their world-famous male voice choir for a few pints and a sing-song. No evening was complete without Tony being asked to give them his version of the Tom Jones hit, *Delilah*."

Cordle – who was known as 'TC' or 'Speedy'- certainly wasn't in the mood for singing during the final throes of Nottinghamshire's innings at St Helen's. He had endured a frustrating first day and was looking forward to putting his feet up after a long spell in the field. Having replaced Ossie Wheatley at the Mumbles Road End, Cordle had opened with a maiden but was taken off after conceding nine runs in his second over. When he returned to the attack as the total approached 250, he was hit for 15 runs by Graham Frost in his third and final over.

"I didn't speak to Malcolm at all during his last over," recalls Cordle, now living in semi-retirement in Canada. "Most of us were out on the boundary and we just left him to carry on with it. As we waited for the balls to come back, Malcolm stood there with his hands on his hips. Some of us were urging him to carry on but you couldn't give him any advice. He wouldn't have taken it anyway – he was such a confident guy."

"It didn't matter what Malcolm bowled," recalls Alan Jones, "he always believed he could get wickets. And there was no backing down from Malcolm Nash. Just because Garry had hit him for four sixes, it didn't mean he was going to bowl him a wide ball – he always attacked him because he thought he could get him out. Malcolm thought Garry would mis-hit one – which he did."

"During the over," recalls Nash, "the umpire, Eddie Phillipson, told me to keep going but there was a lot of silence. I was taking a pasting and there weren't too many people rushing up to me and suggesting where I should put the ball. You were left to work these things out yourself."

After Sobers had stopped talking to Eifion Jones, he patted his bat eight times on the crease – rather like a panther pawing the ground before springing into action. His hapless prey prepared to offer up his latest morsel.

"I wonder where Nash is going to bowl this one?" asked BBC Wales commentator, Wilf Wooller.

"His fifth delivery was of an intelligent length and well up to Sobers on the line of the off stump," reported the 1969 *Glamorgan Yearbook*. "It was the kind that might well have been advised by the captain at this stage of the proceedings had the captain been within talking distance, which he certainly was not."

"I just held the fifth ball back a bit," recalls Nash. "It was a little slower. That sounds silly because I wasn't bowling particularly quickly anyway but I just gave it a little more air and dropped it slightly shorter – a bit like Essex's Ray East or Norman Gifford of Worcestershire used to do."

"Malcolm went a little wide of the off stump and this time I tried to hit it over mid-off," says Sobers. "Although I caught it well, I didn't middle it. I didn't get hold of it properly and it went towards long-off."

"The ball connected a little too high up the bat," reported the *Glamorgan Yearbook*, "and there was not quite the power in the shot that Sobers was looking for."

"I deceived Garry in the flight and he got under it," says Nash. "When I saw it going up, I thought to myself: 'that's it! we've got him! he's out!' And lo and behold, he was."

In fact, he was – and he wasn't. Out on the long-off boundary, to the right of the 67 steps, Roger Davis suddenly found himself standing alone in the spotlight. As he started to re-adjust his position, the eyes of St Helen's were on him and all thoughts of the imminent declaration went out of the window. Into his mind came the ball, as it hurtled towards him from Garry Sobers' bat, and, of course, the wall.

"If you field on the boundary," explains Davis, "you usually start walking in slowly from behind the line so that when you're in play, you're just on the line. But, you can see from the BBC Wales footage that I had walked in further than normal and I was standing about three or four feet inside the boundary. I knew that if the ball came towards me and then went over my head, I'd be in no danger of going over the boundary, and if I had to go backwards with the ball, I wouldn't go over the wall but end up just before the boundary line or just over it. The ball went up in the air and it spun because Garry had mis-hit it."

"And that will just carry," predicted Wooler in the BBC Wales commentary box. "No! He's going to be out!"

"It seemed to kind of move around in the air," Davis recalls. "It wasn't like when a ball is hit flat and it comes straight at you and you line it up so I was thrown a little. I wasn't sure whether it was going to come down quickly or float over my head. I caught it in front of me at chest height but I knew I was off balance because the force of the ball knocked me back a bit."

"Oh! He's dropped it – he's over the boundary!" exclaimed Wooler.

"You couldn't get a better catcher than Roger," recalls Brian Lewis, "and when he fell over I thought 'Oh Roger – what have you done? You could have made a better effort than that!' but I didn't realise how close he was to the line. I didn't join in the discussions but stayed out on the mid-wicket boundary because there was nothing I could do. I let all the senior players do all the talking!"

"From my position at slip," says Majid Khan, "I vividly remember Roger catching the fifth one. We all thought 'Thank God!' but he fell over the white line – according to the people who were sitting behind him in the enclosure."

"If I had been more confident about not going over the wall," recalls Davis, "I would probably have stepped back a little but I started to fall early with the ball in my hands to make sure that I didn't go over the wall. I caught the ball cleanly, fell down and got up. I didn't know where I'd landed."

And as Davis lay on the ground for that split second, therein lay the problem – and ultimately the key to the legality of the six sixes. Where precisely had he landed? Nobody seemed to know, least of all the fielder himself, judging by the querulous, plaintive gesture he immediately made to umpire Eddie Phillipson as he rose to his feet. A more pressing question was immediately asked by everyone in the ground: was Sobers out? Again, nobody seemed to know – apart from a few players and Wilf Wooller. By this time, the man with the mike was in a bit of a tizz.

"Now where are my glasses?" he demanded. "Somebody's pinched my glasses. Let's have a look…Roger Davis caught it but he doesn't know whether he fell over the boundary or not. The umpire's going across to have a look. He's not allowed to go over that boundary line with the ball in his hands – he has to stay this side of it. They're clarifying the position."

Indeed they were – or at least they were trying to. Everybody was having a look: the crowd, the players and especially the umpires. On the square, Sobers had set off on the long journey back to the pavilion. Having seen Davis catch the ball, he assumed his super-quick innings was over.

"I couldn't see what had happened on the boundary from where I was so I started to walk," he recalls. "I was quite willing to go – the six sixes thing didn't make any difference to me because if I was out, I was out and I was on my way – as I always was when I played cricket. If I knew I'd hit the ball, I walked. It didn't matter whether I had 100 runs or 10. But then the crowd started shouting 'you're not out! you're not out! get back! get back!" So I stopped because it looked a little bit funny and the umpire told me to hold on. So I did and waited for a little while."

In fact, it took nearly two minutes for the situation to be resolved. As Phillipson tried to establish what had happened, Sobers stood alongside his ostensible partner, John Parkin, and Nash at the bowler's end. Leaning on his bat, Parkin then started to practise a shot, hoping against hope that he would soon be given the chance to play it for real. He appeared oblivious to the drama unfolding all around him.

Nash was obviously delighted to see Davis take the catch. He felt his initial switch to spin had been vindicated and the more recent change of tactic had worked. The slightly slower ball had done the trick and The Great Man was out. It may have cost 24 runs but that was a small price to pay for the most sought after scalp in the game.

"I breathed a sign of relief," recalls Nash, "but there was pandemonium because nobody knew exactly what was going on. Tony Cordle was saying it was out, a section of the crowd were shouting 'six!', another section were shouting 'out!' Garry thought he was out, I did too and I said to him 'Gotcha!' We were both smiling."

"It didn't matter to me whether Roger caught the ball or not," says Sobers. "I was someone who never played for records and it wouldn't have mattered if I'd got the world record or not. I knew that Roger had caught the ball and I was on my way to the pavilion. Whatever happened after that was out of my control. The umpires were the sole judge of that."

"The roar of anticipation for a fifth six," according to the *Glamorgan Yearbook,* "now changed into one of approval for the splendid catch but this in turn was turned into indecision as umpire Phillipson moved slowly across to enquire from the fielder as to what exactly had occurred. 'A six' chanted some members, 'a catch' called others but I fancy there was a majority opinion in favour of another six."

"After I caught the ball," says Davis, "I couldn't understand what the fuss was about. I thought it was out. 'Speedy' Cordle came across from long-on and said to me: 'That's out – no problem.'

"We discussed it and then Eddie Phillipson the umpire came towards me and asked me if I'd caught it. 'Yes I did,' I replied.

"'Did you go over the boundary?'

"'I don't know. I caught it inside, and got up.'"

And that was the all important question which Phillipson and his fellow umpire, John Langridge, now had to quickly answer: had Roger Davis gone over the boundary while making the catch? Phillips and Langridge had been on the first-class umpires list for 12 years having enjoyed successful careers with Lancashire and Sussex respectively either side of the Second World War. Phillipson, who died in 1991, was a genuine all-rounder – a fast-medium opening bowler and a solid, reliable, middle-order batsman – while Langridge was regarded by many people as the best opening batsman never to have played for England. Between 1928 and 1955, he scored 76 centuries – eight of them double hundreds – and he remains 41st in the all-time run-scoring list. Glamorgan's Alan Jones is the only other non-Test player above him. Both umpires stood in Tests and when Langridge died in 1999, his *Wisden* obituary contained the observation that 'as he aged, his complexion grew more apple-red and he seemed, along-side Sam Cook, [the Gloucestershire bowler who also became an umpire] to represent everything that was best about county cricket.'

During his time as an umpire, Phillipson gained, then revelled in and later boasted about his reputation for giving an excessive number of lbw decisions. Indeed, when Sussex's England bowler, Ian Thomson, went out into the field, he would always throw a piece of grass up into the air and choose his end – depending on the direction in which the grass had been blown. But if Phillipson was standing, it didn't matter which way the wind was blowing: "I'm going to Eddie's end," he would say.

But it was a very different kind of decision that Phillipson had to make during the match between Glamorgan and Nottinghamshire. After a short discussion with Davis and Cordle near the scene of the catch, he decided to confer with

Langridge who was standing, not at square leg but at point, not too far away from Don Shepherd. As his colleague strode towards him, Langridge, white flat cap covering his bald pate and hands firmly clasped behind his back, scurried across the square to their rendezvous at wide mid-off. They were two men in white coats in the middle of a muddle, trying to make sense of a split second of confusion.

"This is the most chaotic situation for a cricket field," declared Wilf Wooller, now having found his glasses. "And nobody seems to know. If the umpire is in doubt, he'll have to give the batsman the benefit of the doubt."

During their mini-conference, Phillipson and Langridge presumably talked about the laws of the game – and, in particular, the new one covering a fair catch which the MCC had only introduced as an experiment that very season. In 1967's *Wisden*, Law 35 stated that 'the fielder must have both his feet entirely within the play area at the instant the catch is completed.' So a year earlier, Sobers would have been adjudged out because Davis' feet were both within the field of play when he took the catch. But the amended version in 1968's *Wisden* declared that 'the fieldsman must have no part of his body grounded outside the playing area in the act of making the catch *and afterwards*.' The addition of those two crucial words meant that Sobers was not out. Wilf Wooller was right. The West Indian captain had scored another six runs because of Davis' movements immediately after catching the ball just inside the boundary. Phillipson walked away from Langridge as Davis waited at long-off for the verdict. By this time, Shepherd had wandered in to provide some sympathy and support for Nash but Phillipson still seemed unsure.

"This is really one of the bits of drama that will be worth looking at again sometime," proclaimed Wooller. "And if there's any doubt, Sobers remains in my view. Now the players are joining in."

As Phillipson deliberated, Walker came across from mid-on to offer his opinion and Tony Lewis began to speak to the umpire. He may have cared little for cricket records but the Glamorgan skipper knew the laws of the game backwards.

"I thought it was not out straightaway because the law had been changed that season," he recalls. "I was sure because I'd sat on the Lord's committee which changed it. If you caught the ball and fell over the line it was six but it hadn't been the year before."

Seconds after speaking to Lewis, Phillipson turned abruptly towards the pavilion, moved his hands from his hips and pointed skywards to indicate his final decision to the scorers. Not so much the slow finger as the very quick pair of arms.

"Six it is!" cried Wooller in the BBC Wales commentary box.

"Four on the trot!" he exclaimed. After pausing to re-count, he tried again.

"Five on the trot!" and then just to make sure he had got it right, "five on the trot!"

But did umpire Phillipson, with the assistance of his colleague Langridge, actually get it right? They were obviously aware of the new law but how, without the help of the plethora of television cameras and slow-motion replays used in modern cricket to analyse such contentious moments, could they possibly have known if Davis had crossed the boundary line? A heated debate continued at the ground after the game but the umpires confirmed their decision. The fielder himself is still not sure what precisely happened after he caught one of the most famous 'catches' in cricket.

"Nobody knew if I'd gone over the line although I must admit that the supporters behind me in the members' enclosure were saying it was six. But they wanted it to be six!" says Davis. "They didn't care about me catching the ball. It may well be that they knew the rule had changed but I didn't and neither did Speedy. I know now it was an experimental rule change. I don't know how the umpires came to their decision. Who decided I had gone over the boundary? I think because there was doubt about whether I had or not, the umpires gave Garry the benefit of it. As far as I'm concerned, I caught the ball and that's good enough for me. The only person who would have known whether I was over the boundary would have been Speedy."

"Roger took the catch but he fell back," recalls Cordle, who was standing in line with Davis at long-on. "The top half of his body went over the line – his back was resting on it – but when he got up, he was still in the field of play. All he was saying when I went to see him was that he had caught the ball."

"If I had my time again," says Davis, "I'd have probably stayed on my feet. I just went with it because I wanted to hit the ground before I hit the wall. If that catch had been a vital part of the game – like the one to win the match – I would have attacked the ball more and made sure I caught it above my head."

On the pavilion roof, the injured Ossie Wheatley and the Nottinghamshire players had enjoyed an exceptional view of the incident. Mike Smedley, the last batsman out, was sitting with his wife, Shelley, who had come down to Swansea for the weekend.

"As Roger caught the ball," he says, "he fell over the line – I'm convinced of that. I immediately thought that it was a six because I knew about the experimental law change. I would think some of the Welsh supporters were biased in wanting a wicket but there were quite a few calling for a six because they probably were aware of the new rule."

"Half the Glamorgan members were hanging out of the windows of the clubhouse telling Garry to go back," recalls Bob White. "That's how keen they were for him to hit six sixes."

"Looking at the replays which I've seen on TV over the

years," says Graham Frost, "I think they confirm that Roger definitely fell over the line. It was a close call but I think he did. I didn't know the law had been changed that year so initially I thought it was out."

"After catching the ball, Roger then fell back over the line," confirms Ossie Wheatley. "It could have been argued that he controlled it enough before he stepped back to claim it as a catch under the old rule but the new one meant you had to have it totally under control while making the catch and afterwards. In most of these great sporting events, there's usually an element of something totally unusual which influences the final outcome."

"Looking back," reflects Davis, "and having seen the footage of the catch and the umpires conferring with no video evidence, it's a strange decision isn't it? I don't want to put it any stronger than that because in a way, it's a part of history and I'm part of it and I'm not going to knock that. Can we tell from the footage whether I was over the boundary? I look very close to it but the camera was not in line. I positioned myself so I wouldn't go over the boundary because of the wall but it may well be that an elbow might have touched the line. I accept that if I fell over the line then it was six."

"I had no idea what happened," says Nash. "I was 50 yards away. If Roger didn't know, how was I to know? My recollection was that Roger actually caught it on his haunches – that is, in a squatting position – inside the line, stumbled, lost his balance and sat down with his backside on the line. He had control of the ball, it was gripped in his hands and he then got up. The 1968 law change proved very significant and as Wilf said in his commentary, when in doubt, the benefit goes to the batsman."

The experimental rule was later ratified and has remained largely unaltered, apart from minor modifications, for the last 40 years. Law 32.4 states that "six runs shall be scored if a fielder (i) has any part of his person touching the boundary or grounded beyond the boundary when he catches the ball or (ii) catches the ball and subsequently touches the boundary or grounds some part of his person over the boundary while carrying the ball but before completing the catch."

The rule that has remained resolutely unchanged since the original cricket code was drawn up in 1744 is the current Law 3.7 which states that "the umpires shall be the sole judges of fair and unfair play."

It may have seemed a rather harsh decision not to dismiss Sobers – particularly on the unfortunate Nash who, at last, had managed to induce a mis-hit – but it was fair and it was final. Once it had been made, the verdict was greeted by a huge cheer – and a few barely audible boos – and Sobers broke away from a conversation he was having with Cordle to head back down the wicket to the Mumbles Road End.

As the Glamorgan players and the two officials returned to their positions, the Nottinghamshire captain shot a grateful glance to the heavens before his famous cheek-to-cheek grin lit up his face. The gods were indeed smiling on Garry Sobers. The greatest cricketer in the world was now standing on the brink of immortality. Nobody had ever hit six sixes in an over before and history was his for the taking. Five down, one to go. Those extra 30 runs had taken the Nottinghamshire captain on to 70 and his team to a massive 388. Superman needed to deliver a superball if the names of Sobers and Nash were not to be joined irrevocably together for the rest of their lives.

THE SIXTH BALL

Malcolm Nash couldn't leap over tall buildings in a single bound or lift a car over his head but he did have something in common with Superman: on his day, he could be pretty quick.

Perhaps not "faster than a speeding bullet", as Clark Kent invariably became when in possession of his costume and cape, but quick enough to later earn himself an England Test trial and cause havoc among some of the best opening batsmen in English county cricket.

So when Eddie Phillipson signalled the fifth sixth in what proved to be the final over of the Nottinghamshire innings, Nash decided to go back to doing what he did best. There was no alternative. It was time for the spinning to stop, he had to revert to the tried and tested. The experiment was over. It had worked wonders at first but it was fast turning into the bowling spell from hell. He knew he had one last chance to capture the wicket of the biggest name in the game and it was all or nothing.

"When the six was given after Roger had caught Garry on the boundary," says Nash, "I felt deflated but I had already made up my mind when I was walking back to bowl that the last ball was going to be a seamer. I was definitely going to bowl a quicker one. I was going through the same thought process as I had throughout the over: I was trying to get him out. And I still felt that Garry Sobers' wicket on my resume would have been really good."

As Nash prepared to bowl the final ball, Peter Walker, as an orthodox left-arm spinner himself, realised what was going on. From his position at mid-on, the all-rounder had the best seat in the house. He was perfectly placed to notice that Nash was at last getting a grip.

"Malcolm changed from holding the ball across the seam like you do for spin and instead had the seam pointing towards the batsman," says Walker. "This is the normal orthodox seam bowler's position so that when the ball lands, the seam is at right angles to the ground. That indicated to me that Malcolm wasn't going to let the sixth one go at the slowish medium-pace he had bowled the other balls. He was going to go back to his basic skill of bowling fast-medium with the seam straight up rather than at an angle to the line of the bowler's fingers. The action is diametrically opposed to bowling spin and the change back was too drastic and sudden to guarantee accuracy."

Garry Sobers didn't need to see Nash's new grip at such close quarters to realise that something was afoot. He anticipated that the bowler would try to change tack and his vast experience of playing cricket around the world meant he knew what to expect.

"When the umpire signalled a six off the fifth ball," recalls Sobers, "I thought it didn't matter where Malcolm pitched the last one – I was going to try and hit it for six. I knew he was going to try to trick me because, as a spinner myself, I knew that when you're bowling slowly and getting a bit of stick, you slip a quicker one in. When he turned to walk back and prepared to bowl the final ball, I knew what was coming so I was ready for him."

"There was a hell of a buzz in the ground then," says Roger Davis. "I was more concerned about a declaration because I was going to be opening the batting. The fact that it could be six sixes wasn't really going through my mind."

As Sobers tapped his bat on the crease 13 times, Phillipson, Eifion Jones and Majid Khan resumed their positions. The non-striker, John Parkin, at last seemed resigned to the fact that there was no point in looking for a run. Everybody in the ground knew where the next ball was going.

"It was only after the fifth ball that I thought I could hit six sixes," says Sobers. "I wanted to try and make sure that if I did get the record, it was going to be clean. I wanted it to be unique without a no-ball or a wide involved."

"By the fifth six," recalls Don Shepherd, 'I thought 'My God, if that's gone, then there's a real chance of him hitting six!' and Garry was bound to play a shot on the last ball. While we were waiting around for the umpires to decide on Roger's catch, I wandered over to speak to Malcolm. 'Pitch it up, get it under the bat and he can't hit you for six,' I said. It was just something I would have said to whoever was bowling."

"One of my thoughts as Malcolm prepared to bowl that ball," recalls Tony Cordle, "was that a six would probably shut him up because he always fancied himself as a left-arm spinner. My other thought was that if Garry smacked the ball over the boundary then we were going to be witnessing history."

"Five on the trot," said Wilf Wooller in the BBC Wales commentary box. "This is incredible. Six on the trot is a world record. Seventy on the board."

"It was clear to even the most unlikely follower of records," reported the 1969 *Glamorgan Yearbook*, "that a world record was at stake, since no one could hit more than six sixes off six balls. The crowd awaited expectantly. The fielders spread even deeper and there was a quiet tension in the air."

Like everyone else in the ground, Nash knew that Sobers would be trying to hit a six. He realised he needed a special delivery to avoid becoming the fall guy in one of cricket's most celebrated double acts.

"I was determined that he wasn't going to hit this one for six," says Nash, "but to bowl him a seamer off a short run was not a very good idea because my rhythm had gone. And it was the worst ball of the over. It was awful. I tried to bowl a quick ball and produced a half-tracker."

The report in the *Glamorgan Yearbook* was a shade kinder to Nash. "The last spinner was a little bit short on the leg-side but might, under other circumstances, have been played for four runs but Sobers let it go. It was the least correct stroke of the over."

"Everybody's feeling was that Garry was a great cricketer," says Alan Jones. "He was the best certainly I ever played against and deep down, I wanted him to hit the final ball for six."

"Malcolm came up in his normal slow left-arm spin style," recalls Sobers, "and, all of a sudden, he flattened it out. Unfortunately for him, he dropped it half way down the wicket. I was seeing it as big as a football by this time and I had one eye on the ball and the other eye on the short boundary on the leg-side and when I hit it, I caught it right in the middle of the bat. Even if I had top-edged it, the ball would have gone for six."

"It was a rank long hop," admits Nash. "It was totally unintentional and it disappeared for many a mile – Garry hit it to Timbuktu. I was absolutely silly. I should have been bowling over not round the wicket. He was a very good player off the back foot – period. He could play even a half-volley off the back foot."

"The bat swung from the outside line of the off-stick to mid-wicket," reported the *Glamorgan Yearbook*, "and with it the ball flew like an arrow, past the scoreboard, where it disappeared at some considerable velocity over the wall and down St Helen's Avenue as the crowd erupted in a tremendous roar of approval and applause."

"It was a hell of a shot which went to my right over Alan Rees' head at mid-wicket," recalls Alan Jones. "It was brilliant, the crowd just went mad – it was a heck of a feat."

"And he's done it!," cried Wooller. "And my goodness, it's gone way down to Swansea!"

Then, after a brief pause for breath, Wooller composed himself and delivered the final comments of an exhilarating five minutes in front of the microphone.

"Six on the trot, 36 in one over, my goodness gracious! What a moment! What a batsman!"

There was a similar feeling of elation and wonderment both inside the BBC Wales scanner and on the camera gantry as the event was recorded for posterity.

"As the over unfolded, I was just excited," recalled director John Norman. "We were seeing some great batting – it was as simple as that. Wilf was usually unflappable but he got progressively more excited so that by the time of the last ball, he was nearly hysterical."

"As the last ball was about to be bowled," said cameraman John Lewis, "I thought to myself that I must catch this one. Garry gave it such a clout that it went right over the boundary, out of the ground and down the road. I'm not sure whether the ball was in the camera frame but at least people could see where it had gone. It was going so fast it was difficult to follow. I was very relieved that I'd managed at least to follow the ball as much as I could. I was only aware afterwards that I was filming history – not at the time."

"When Wilf cried 'it's gone way down to Swansea!'", recalled Norman, "we were all standing up and cheering in the van. I wasn't aware that it was history in the making until it was all over. I rang *Grandstand* to tell them we had six sixes which I didn't think had been done before – I didn't honestly know if it had – and that we had them on tape in Cardiff. I could hear the tremendous excitement in London over the phone but I could also hear the closing *Grandstand* music so I knew they couldn't get the action into the programme. The *Grandstand* editor, Brian Cowgill, said they would open their Sunday programme with the six sixes the next day and we were to get post-match interviews – all the usual thing."

"It was a natural reaction for Malcolm to want to put the last delivery through a bit quicker," says Shepherd. "When the ball went out of the ground, I felt it couldn't have happened to a nicer bloke than Garry – there was no anti-feeling whatsoever."

As the ball disappeared in the rough direction of the city centre, the Glamorgan players applauded and Sobers modestly wandered down the wicket for a spot of gardening before raising his bat with his right hand in brief acknowledgement of the tumultuous reception he was receiving from the St Helen's crowd. When it was obvious that, unlike the first two balls of the over, the sixth wasn't about to be returned, the umpires had to confer again. With neither Phillipson nor Langridge having a replacement on them, Sobers decided it was time to call it a day. Down at the other end, John Parkin finally accepted that the game was up; his chance to get on strike and help move the score along had come – and gone.

"I knew that wherever the last ball was pitched," he recalls, "it was going to go in the air and be caught or go for six. I couldn't say I kept thinking that it would be a world record and that would be the end of the innings because I thought Garry would go on for another over – having said we'd have another 10 minutes. 'Well done skipper,' I said as he walked towards me. 'Come on, let's go,' he replied. 'That's enough.'"

Mission accomplished. The quick runs Sobers had wanted had been scored, probably a little faster than expected, and it was time for Glamorgan to bat.

"I didn't really intend to declare then," says Sobers, "but when I realised we couldn't get the ball back for the next over, I felt we were wasting time so the best thing was to declare the innings so we could get the new ball to bowl with. I probably would have gone on for another over but after the time was lost by the ball being in the road, I thought that, to quicken the game, to keep it moving, the best thing to do was declare."

In doing so, Sobers forsook the chance not only to improve on the record he had already set for the quickest hundred of the season but to pick up 100 guineas (£105) by winning *The People's* six-hit championship. At that late stage of the season, he was level with Essex's Lee Irvine on 25 each and the South African went on to pip by him by one because Sobers' 72 in Nottinghamshire's second innings at Swansea contained no sixes. But, as usual, records were the last thing on his mind as, to a standing ovation, he made his way back to the visitors' dressing room to be met by a chorus of congratulations from most of his team-mates.

"It was then that I fully appreciated what had happened," says Parkin. "I had been part of something I'd never have thought I would have been involved in. It was then that it sank in that Garry had set a world record. But he didn't do anything in particular afterwards. For him, it was just another day at the office."

"I thought Garry must have been on for the fastest hundred of the season," says middle-order batsman Mike Smedley. "He already held the record of 77 minutes and he'd scored 76 in 35 minutes so it must have been on but he decided to declare to keep the game going. Most of the shots would have been sixes on any other county ground because he hit the ball so hard and so far. Afterwards, Garry didn't say anything. He was a pretty modest, humble chap and he just saw it as part of a team effort. He wanted to get on with the rest of the game but everybody was chuffed to bits that he'd done it and that it had happened to such a nice person."

"It was magnificent, unbelievable," says wicket-keeper Deryck Murray. "It had never been done before so you never imagined that it would be done. We were all out there cheering with everybody else – we tended to watch whenever Garry went out to bat because something special was likely to happen."

"It's a tremendous feat to hit six sixes because you can always mis-hit one can't you?" says Graham Frost. "What was in Garry's favour was that he was a left-hander and Nash was bowling from the wrong end because he'd got the very short boundary to his left. But that doesn't diminish the achievement: you've still got to do it, you've got to produce the goods. The crowd were so appreciative, I remember they were still clapping after we'd declared, had the break and come back out to bowl."

Sobers might have made history with probably the most extraordinary innings ever seen in English county cricket but his achievement didn't cut much ice with one of his teammates. The late David Halfyard was a former Kent seamer who had been forced to retire from the game in 1962 after being badly injured in a car crash. He became a first-class umpire and whilst officiating at Trent Bridge, had been spotted bowling in the nets. He ended up being signed by Nottinghamshire but not before almost the whole committee had spent two hours watching him in action to make sure he was fit. The 1968 season was the first of three he spent at Trent Bridge and according to opening batsman Bob White, Halfyard believed his captain had made a grave error by not batting on at Swansea.

"Garry couldn't be bothered to see Eddie Phillipson stagger up those 70-odd steps at St Helen's to get another ball so he declared," says White. "But when he got back in the dressing room, Dave, a real old pro, went absolutely ballistic. He tore into Garry, saying we should have carried on batting and claiming that we'd thrown away a winning position. 'I couldn't be bothered to wait for another ball,' said Garry and he had the last laugh because we went on to win the game and Dave had to concede that there were more ways of playing a game of cricket than the old pro's way."

"As I walked off the field with Garry," Nash recalls, "he said words to the effect of 'Hey…well bowled – bad luck. It was my day.' I was smiling through shell-shock – not because he'd created a world record. Obviously history had just been made but what was I going to do: sit down in the middle of the pitch and cry?"

When the players reached the Glamorgan dressing room, the mood was a mixture of commiseration and ironic congratulation. Having taken a pounding out on the pitch from Sobers, Nash knew he would be subjected to similar treatment from his team-mates. Light-hearted banter was flying around all over the place as they took the Michael out of Malcolm.

"As a fellow bowler," says Ossie Wheatley, "I felt huge sympathy for him because he wasn't bowling normally but, at the same time, I think I realised what it would mean to him. 'You can dine out on this for ever,' I said to him straight after the game. 'This is one of the great cricket stories.'"

"My team mates didn't quite know what to say to me," remembers Nash, "but Tony Lewis was pretty astute. He said I should make sure I got the right fees from the press for talking to them about the over. Then somebody suggested I could write a book about it. 'What would you call it, Nashy?' piped up Tony Cordle. '*Gone with the Wind*?!'"

As Alan Jones and Roger Davis were putting on their pads in the Glamorgan dressing room, most of the county's supporters were still trying to come to terms with the historic event they had just witnessed. Not surprisingly, it was the sole topic of conversation around St Helen's – from the members' enclosure in front of the pavilion to the Gorse Lane side of the ground and down to the Mumbles Road End. Pat Hughes, a Glamorgan member since 1949, was sitting about five rows from the front of the enclosure near the bottom of the 67 steps when the famous over began. As a result, she had an excellent view of the disputed fifth six when Roger Davis caught the ball before falling over the boundary.

"I'd been in no danger from the third one which went right over my head and I thought Roger had the ball in his hand when he went over the line," she recalls. "I would have liked to think Garry was out but I was convinced it was a six because Roger had gone over the line. I didn't know the rule change in any great detail but I was aware that if he went over the boundary in the process of catching the ball then he would be out.

"It was incredible. Everything else was overshadowed by the six sixes. I don't think any of us realised, even after the sixth six, quite what a momentous occasion it was. I can remember the excitement of watching this amazing batsman hammering poor old Malcolm and realising afterwards that this was really quite something – but not realising it at the time.

"Before the final ball, I think we all secretly hoped that Garry would do it. We wanted to be there for that occasion. We all felt sorry for Malcolm, knowing that he would go down for ever in history as the bowler, but I think with Garry having got the five, most people in their heart of hearts wanted him to do it. When he did, we all jumped up and shouted 'wow!' I'm just pleased that I can say 'I was there'."

Another long-standing supporter sitting in the members' enclosure that day was John Williams, the current chairman of the St Helen's Balconiers. This group of loyal spectators generally sat in a corner of the original pavilion balcony – hence their name – and they set up the association in 1972, in the wake of the then record opening partnership of 330 between Alan Jones (105) and Roy Fredericks (228 not out). Although the initial aim was to donate money towards a man-of-the-match award at games held at St Helen's, more than £175,000 has been raised in the last 10 years as part of a campaign to keep Glamorgan cricket in Swansea.

"In the morning, I'd been sitting on one of the balconies," recalls Williams, "and I distinctly remember seeing Garry Sobers playing the one-armed bandits in the club and going down to a bookies not far from the ground in King Edward's Road during the lunch interval.

"The beauty about Sobers as a player was that he was so athletic. Whether bowling, batting or fielding, he did it with so much rhythm. The first four sixes were beautiful strokes and then we had the one that Roger caught on the boundary.

I was sitting right behind him and he definitely fell over the line with the ball. The sixes happened so fast that we didn't realise that history had been made. When the last ball went out of the ground, it took a few minutes to sink in. I count myself to have been very lucky to have been there on that historic occasion."

In the early 1980s, John Williams and The Balconiers took over the running of a beer and tea bar at the Mumbles Road End of St Helen's which had been operated by Fred Jenkins until his death. Fred's Shed became Fred's Bar and a regular source of income for The Balconiers. During the game against Nottinghamshire in 1968, Emlyn Lake, from Penllergaer in Swansea, had taken up a position near Fred's Shed – not far from the end of the rugby grandstand.

"I missed the morning session but arrived at St Helen's in the afternoon," he recalls. "Sobers came in a place or two down from his normal batting position and it was a joy to see his relaxed style of playing but he was soon in a punishing mood. After the third ball, the spectators were starting to get very excited and after the fourth and fifth balls were treated in the same manner, the excitement reached fever pitch. We all knew that if the sixth ball was to be hit with the same force as the previous five, we'd be witnessing an historic moment in the game. I felt privileged to be present on such a unique occasion. Like everyone else, I marvelled at such an exhibition of aggressive batting but I also had a degree of sympathy for the bowler."

Not far from Fred's Shed, Alun Harries, from Manselton in Swansea, was sitting in a garden chair on a patch of grass between the end of the rugby grandstand and the sightscreen. A Glamorgan supporter since 1947, he had been at St Helen's from the start of play and remembers the history-making over well.

"When the fourth and the fifth balls went for six," he says, "people started asking whether it was going to be a record –

although I wasn't aware that five sixes were the most that had been hit off an over. I had seen people hit three in an over before and the former Glamorgan wicketkeeper, Haydn Davies, was a six-and-out chap – he hit a few sixes in his day – but Sobers' shots were tremendous. The only short one was the one that Roger Davis caught, the others went miles up in the air. At the time, I didn't think it was all that important but looking back on it 40 years later, I'm glad to be able to say that I was there."

So is Richard Lewis, now a history and politics teacher at Bournville School in Birmingham but then a 17-year-old schoolboy and self-confessed cricket fanatic from Pontardawe. In the aftermath of the historic over, he was about to take a short walk which would lead to his unlikely inclusion in the cast of characters involved in the six sixes story. Lewis had gone to the game with his family – including his late father, Charles and his late brother, John, who was then 15.

"We were sitting on seats on the concrete terracing on the Gorse Lane side of the ground and we had the scoreboard on our right." he recalls. "It was only from the third six that you began to see that a record could be on. The last shot sailed out of the ground and about three or four minutes after Garry Sobers had declared, my father suggested that I should go and see if I could find the ball. So off I went by myself down St Helen's Avenue and there it was for all to see! I was full of the pleasure and the excitement of the occasion, of seeing Garry perform that wonderful scoring feat, and there was the ball in the road. So, straightaway, there was a link that would be there forever."

Lewis picked up the ball, put it in his pocket and rushed back to his father who, like him, was thrilled by his discovery. After watching Glamorgan stagger to 77 for three at the close, they packed up their belongings and went home to Pontardawe. But after a family conference that evening, Charles Lewis rang the cricket club at St Helen's the next day and offered to return to the ball.

"We obviously thought it was a wonderful memento of this fabulous record," recalls Richard Lewis, "but, thinking about it that evening, we felt it was the right thing to hand it back. Although it was very tempting to keep the ball, we decided it should go back to its proper place with Garry Sobers. It was only right that his feat should be remembered in this manner."

So, before play started on the last day of the game, Lewis handed over his most prized possession to Sobers at St Helen's. In return, he received a replacement ball signed by the West Indies captain. The original was destined for the Trent Bridge museum in Nottingham.

While the Lewis family travelled back to Pontardawe after the game on the Saturday, the press were obviously looking for some post-event reaction and Malcolm Nash didn't let them down.

"I could see I was in trouble after I had bowled the first two balls," he told *The Western Mail*. "When the fourth went for six, it was also very obvious that Sobers was out for the record. It was very difficult to know what to bowl to him when he was in such an aggressive mood. He was absolutely merciless but I was one of the first to congratulate him on a marvellous display."

"I'm shattered – as any bowler would be," Nash confessed to *The People*. "It seems ironical that I've been contributed to a world record but what a player this man his. Frankly, it's an honour just to be playing against him."

Tony Lewis told the assembled scribes that the record had not been achieved by "sheer slogging through strength, but well-controlled scientific hitting with every movement working in harmony. One shot which sent the ball out of the ground was actually made off the back foot."

Sobers himself was less forthcoming about his performance – as the reporter from *The People* simply stated:

"The message came back from a firmly shut dressing room door. 'He has no wish to discuss this innings with the Press. They saw what happened and that stands for itself.'"

But the Nottinghamshire captain was in a much more relaxed mood when he was interviewed with Nash by BBC Wales reporter Brian Hoey on the television gantry down at the Mumbles Road End at close of play.

"As we walked across the field to do the interview," Sobers recalls, "out of the corner of my eye, I caught Malcolm smiling to himself. When I asked him why he seemed so perky for a man who'd just been hit for a world record, he said: 'I'm in the record books too... I want you to remember that you couldn't have done it without me!'"

During the interview, Sobers, casually smoking a cigarette alongside the still smiling Nash, re-iterated the philosophy which he pursued throughout his 20 years at the top of the game. After introducing the pair as "the vanquished and the victor", Hoey asked Sobers if there had been any point in the over, particularly after the first two or three sixes, when he thought that he would go for a world record?

"No, not really," replied Sobers. "I'm not one of those players who concentrates on records or averages, as one might think. I just play the game and whatever comes along, comes along. The only time I thought about hitting six sixes was the last ball when I thought if I'd hit five, I might as well try for the other one."

After asking a couple of questions about Sobers' decision to walk having been 'caught' off the fifth ball, and his subsequent declaration, Hoey then turned to Nash, who was sitting to Sobers' right on the television gantry.

"Malcolm, up until this fateful over for you, you were bowling extremely well. Your figures were four for 64 – how do you feel after it?"

"As you say," replied Nash, "up until that one over, things were going quite well. It's the first time that I've bowled spin this year and I was quite pleased with the success. And then Garry, who was in such an aggressive mood, just sought me out. He hit me. They weren't slogs – he just played tremendous cricket."

"Were you feeling completely demoralised after the innings?", continued Hoey.

"No I wasn't – strangely enough. I felt that I would very much like to carry on bowling and try to capture his wicket."

Bloodied but unbowed, Superman's self-confidence, if not his bowling analysis, was still intact. Those 36 runs had taken him to an unwanted century and produced final figures of 21-5-100-4. For the record, Glamorgan were bowled out for 254, with Majid Khan making 41 and Peter Walker 104 not out, before Nottinghamshire declared at 139 for six, Sobers top-scoring with 72, and then dismissed the home side for 113 to win the match by 166 runs. Nottinghamshire finished fourth in the championship, a place behind Glamorgan, and Sobers duly collected his champagne from Bunty Ames.

By the time Sobers' achievement had been beamed around the world, having featured heavily in the Sunday edition of *Grandstand*, the previous record holder, Arthur Wellard, had been contacted for his reaction to the news. Thirty years after he had smacked five successive sixes off a Frank Woolley over at Wells, the former Somerset allrounder added his profuse congratulations.

"It is a great feat," he declared. "Even on the smallest ground, sixes want hitting and to hit six of them in an over is wonderful."

In the 1969 *Glamorgan Yearbook*, the author of the special report on the over had been moved to enlist the support of Shakespeare's oft-quoted line from *Twelfth Night*: "Be not afraid of greatness: some are born great, some achieve greatness and some have greatness thrust upon them" but he ended up misquoting him.

"The names of Nash and Sobers are indissolubly linked for ever and a day," he wrote. "'Some,' the Bard said dear Malcolm, 'have fame thrust upon them.'"

Garry Sobers was not born great but he achieved greatness and Malcolm Nash had greatness – or fame – thrust upon him. A unique feat had been performed by a unique cricketer who had set a unique record. It would be 17 years before another batsman would be similarly blessed by the cricketing gods but no subsequent hitting of six sixes in an over would ever be able to match the first one.

HISTORY
REPEATING ITSELF

Ravi Shastri was on a roll. He was having the best season of his career and the time of his life. Whenever the Indian all-rounder went out to bat, he seemed to be in the runs. The opposition and the type of competition appeared irrelevant. In Test matches, first-class games or one-day internationals, Shastri just kept on scoring – at home and abroad. So it was perhaps not surprising that right in the middle of his *annus mirabilis*, he should write his name into cricket's record books – not once but twice in the very same game.

On 10th January 1985, while playing for Bombay against Baroda in the Ranji Trophy, the cricket championship of India, Shastri not only emulated Garry Sobers' feat of hitting six sixes in an over but then went on to score the fastest double hundred in the history of the game.

"It was an unbelievable feeling when the sixth ball smashed into the sightscreen," recalls Shastri, now a television commentator in India. "At the time, I didn't realise what I'd done. It was only after it was in the papers the next day that it finally started sinking in and I understood the magnitude of my performance."

Although he began his career as a left-arm orthodox spinner, Shastri gradually moved up the batting order from tailender to opener as he won 80 Test caps and appeared in 150 one-day internationals. He had been Bombay's youngest debutant when he played against Bihar at the age of 17 years and 292 days in March 1980. A year later, he made his India debut, taking three wickets in four balls in New Zealand's second innings in the first Test in Wellington. In the third Test, his seven wickets won him the man-of-the-match award and his total of 15 in the series was the highest for both sides.

"His calm, sensible batting lower in the order," recorded *Wisden,* "raised promise of his developing into a useful all–rounder, and his fielding too was an asset." Shastri turned from being a lower-order hitter to a more circumspect top-order batsman and he was often criticised for his slow scoring. India's greatest all-rounder, Kapil Dev, once described him as having "50 per cent in cricketing ability but 200 per cent determination."

"I did a lot of bowling in my early days," says Shastri, "but as my career progressed, I really developed as a batsman and for a period of three years in the 1980s, I was a genuine all-rounder. I still bowled but towards the end of my career, my batting took centre stage. I remember that I couldn't do anything wrong in the 1984-85 season – it was a fantastic year."

Shastri's extraordinary run of form began in early October 1984 when he hit 102 against Australia in a one-day international. Later that month, he scored 71 and 139 in successive Test matches against Pakistan, on a tour that was later cancelled because of the assassination of the Indian Prime Minster, Indira Gandhi, before making 142 in the first Test against England at the Wankhede Stadium in Bombay in early December. He scored 102 against England in a one-day international towards the end of the month and then made 111 in the third Test early in the New Year at Eden Gardens in Calcutta. But the innings took seven hours and when he was pelted with fruit by an angry crowd, the riot police had to be called to the ground.

Three days later after the drawn Test in Calcutta, Shastri returned to the Wankhede Stadium for the match against Baroda. Bombay won the toss and decided to bat but he wasn't needed as they made 371 for four declared. Baroda declared 39 runs behind – with Shastri picking up three wickets for 73 runs – and then Bombay set about the opposition's attack. Opener Lalchand Rajput made 136 and skipper Sunny Gavaskar hit 49 but Shastri dominated the innings with 200 not out. Batting at number six, his first hundred came up in 72 minutes and 80 balls and the second took just 41 minutes and 43 balls as he recorded the fastest double hundred in first-class cricket. It had taken 113 minutes, included 13 fours and 13 sixes and beat the previous record – held jointly by Gilbert Jessop on his way to scoring 286 for Gloucestershire in 1903 and Lancashire's Clive Lloyd as he made 201 not out in 1976 – by seven minutes. But it was the six sixes from an over by Tilak Raj which gained him a double entry in the record books as the six foot three all-rounder made spectacular use of his long reach against a fellow left-arm spinner.

"I had reached my first hundred," Shastri recalls, "when a message came from the dressing room that we would be declaring in half an hour or 40 minutes so I decided to really go for it. I remember the over very well. The first one went over long-on, the second a little wider and the third went over mid-off. It was only then that I thought there was no harm in going for the jugular. I had nothing to lose so I'd just go for it. I thought the fourth was the best of the lot because Tilak fired it down the leg-side and I somehow managed to get some bat on it, literally one-handed, and it disappeared over square leg and into the stand. I definitely knew it was 'game on' then because I could see some panic buttons being pressed in the opposition line-up. There were a lot of players going up to Tilak and giving him advice and I just got the feeling that I had a chance."

One of those players was Baroda's captain, Kiran More, who watched Shastri's innings from behind the stumps.

"We tried our best," he says. "Tilak was a smart cricketer who knew his business. He bowled short, down the leg, outside the off stump and a yorker but in vain. It was one of those great innings. Shastri was slogging, improvising and playing some great shots. He hit over mid-on to fine leg and he even played a one-handed shot."

"The fifth one was big," recalls Shastri, "between long-on and mid-wicket and the sixth was pure guess work. There was a lot of time taken before Tilak bowled the last ball because advice was coming from everywhere. It was very clear in my mind that all the pressure was falling on him. I was just trying to guess what he might do. I had to go one way and see if something could be manufactured out of the situation so I decided to step a little bit outside leg stump. I reasoned that if he fired it down the leg-side, I could still reach it and if he went down the off, I could still somehow reach it. If I'd stood where I was and he'd fired it down the leg-side then it could have been a problem. It came off because he actually fired the ball down the off-side, trying to bowl a yorker length just outside the off stump, and, from my position just outside leg stump, I managed to reach it and flat-batted it straight on to the sightscreen.

"Tilak was a fast-ish left-arm spinner who would push the ball through flat and quick. I don't know what happened during the over but now he likes to forget it and I'm not surprised. He said that it shook him mentally and people kept rubbing it in by reminding him of it."

Once Shastri had reached 200, Gavaskar declared the innings on 457 for five and the match was eventually drawn. But the tall all-rounder hadn't finished. Towards the end of the month, he scored 53 in a one-day international against England before going to Australia for the World Championship of Cricket one-day competition in February and March. India won the tournament, which had been created to celebrate the 150th anniversary of the founding of Victoria, and Shastri picked up the man-of-the-series award for his 182 runs and eight wickets. In his last three games, he hit three fifties, including 63 against Pakistan in the eight-wicket win in the final. Shastri then returned to India to help Bombay win the Ranji Trophy by beating Delhi by 90 runs – their 30th victory in the trophy's 50-year history. After taking four wickets in Delhi's first innings, he top-scored with 76 as Bombay set a target of 300 to win in a day and then took eight for 91 to round off a remarkable season.

In 1987, Shastri became the first Indian Test cricketer to play for Glamorgan. While they struggled in championship matches – finishing bottom of the table in two of his four seasons – 1988 proved to be one of their most successful years in terms of the one-day game. They moved up from 14th to fifth in the Sunday League – with Shastri winning the leading six-hitter award with 14 – and reached the semi-finals of the Benson and Hedges Cup where they lost to Derbyshire.

"I had a very enjoyable time with Glamorgan," he recalls. "They were great people, the camaraderie was good and we had a very young team who you saw the best of in the 1990s – especially when they won the Sunday League in 1993, when all the youngsters like Hugh Morris, Matthew Maynard, Robert Croft and Steve Watkin came to the fore, and then the championship in 1997. We struggled a bit in the four-day game but we were a dangerous one-day side and with a little luck, I think we could have won the Benson and Hedges Cup in 1988. The game against Derbyshire at St Helen's which we lost by 14 runs was affected by the weather and I thought we had the team to win the final."

In the same year, Shastri had captained India for the only time when he led them to a 255-run victory in the fourth Test against the West Indies in Madras and during his sabbatical from Glamorgan in 1990, he scored two hundreds against England for the Indian tourists. After making 100 at Lord's, he scored 187 in a marathon innings at The Oval, which prompted journalist Harsha Bhogle to observe:

"For nine hours and 21 minutes, he chiselled away at the England attack and the sculpture that he left behind represented perseverance and craft. There was the usual stoic, expressionless face under the helmet, but you could see the determination in his eyes as he planted himself at the wicket, struck root and bore fruit."

After that innings, Shastri made a career-best 217 for the Rest of India against Bengal in the opening match of the Indian season and in the following year he became Shane Warne's first Test victim when he made 206 in the third Test in Sydney. The trademark innings took nine and a half hours, contained 17 fours and two sixes and contributed to the young leg-spinner's final figures of 45-7-150-1. During that match, the knee injury which would end Shastri's career first became apparent and he retired from the game in 1994 to become a broadcaster with ESPN Star Sports until leaving to commentate on the inaugural Indian Premier League. More than 23 years after scoring his six sixes, he is delighted to share a place in the record books with Garry Sobers.

"While I was still playing, I thought it was OK but I rated my Test achievements higher – Test-match cricket was the ultimate thing for me," reflects Shastri. "But when I finished my career, I started thinking about it and realised that it was an outstanding achievement. To hit six sixes in any form of cricket – I don't care who the bowler is – isn't easy at all and it doesn't happen that often. I'm a little surprised that more people haven't done it when you see the amount of one-day cricket being played. I think it's very tough to do in first-class cricket because a bowler can bowl wide – it has to be a real wide to be called one – whereas in the one-day game, the bowler more or less has to bowl at the stumps."

On the 40th anniversary of the first six sixes, Shastri is rightly proud of his achievement and refutes suggestions that the Bombay versus Baroda game was not as good as Glamorgan's match against Nottinghamshire in 1968.

"I would say the standard was better than an English county game. It was first-class cricket and there were some good international players involved. Look at the record of some of them... Sunny Gavaskar played 125 times for India,

Sandeep Patil won 29 caps, Kiran More made 49 appearances and Mohinder Armanath played 69 times for his country. The standard of Indian first-class cricket was very high at that time."

The same couldn't be said about the quality of cricket being played by the Netherlands when Herschelle Gibbs joined the Six Sixes Club during the World Cup in the West Indies in 2007. The South African batsman had already achieved considerable fame through his prodigious run-scoring and a series of notorious controversies. As well as hitting two double centuries for his country, Gibbs holds the national record partnership of 368 with Graeme Smith and they are the only pair in Test history to have put on 300 together three times. Gibbs is one of only three batsmen to have scored three consecutive hundreds in one-day internationals and his most famous innings was arguably the 175 he hammered in 111 balls when South Africa chased down an improbable 434 with a ball to spare to beat Australia 3-2 in a one-day series in Johannesburg in 2006.

Away from the crease, Gibbs' part in the match-fixing scandal involving the late Hansie Cronje was revealed to the 2000 King Commission inquiry into corruption in South African cricket. Although he admitted agreeing to accept money to score "less than 20" in a one-day international, he actually hit 74 runs and was banned for six months. Gibbs refused to tour the sub-continent for fear of arrest before eventually being interviewed by Indian police six years later. On a West Indies tour in 2001, he was fined for smoking marijuana as some of the South Africans celebrated their Test series win and in January 2007, he received a three-match ban, on appeal, for making racist comments to members of the crowd after team-mate Paul Harris had been abused during the first Test against Pakistan.

Two months later, Gibbs got back to making runs rather than the wrong sort of headlines. In a World Cup group game against the Netherlands on St Kitts on 16th March 2007, he smashed Daan van Bunge for six sixes in an over to become the first batsman to achieve the feat in international cricket. The boundaries may have been short – Warner Park in Basseterre is just a foot over the minimum requirement for an international ground of 140 yards from end to end – and the bowler was a part-time leg-spinner but it was still a remarkable display of hitting.

Before the tournament began, the former West Indies captain, Viv Richards, had expressed the hope that someone would follow in the footsteps of Sobers and Shastri by hitting the perfect six.

"These days, we are seeing more and more big totals and sixes being hit in one-day cricket by powerful batsmen with big bats," he said, "yet no-one has ever hit six sixes in one over of any international match. To me, this tournament, with our traditionally short boundaries, is the time to change that."

The game between South Africa and the Netherlands had been reduced to 40 overs and The Proteas were cruising towards a big total as Smith and Jacques Kallis tore into the bowling. Gibbs joined Kallis at 114 for two and in the 30th over he decided it was time to let loose with a collection of improvised and unconventional shots.

"I had been in for about 10 minutes or so when the message came out that we had to push it on a bit," he recalls. "Jacques and I were told we could have a dip, and we probably had a bigger dip than was needed. I got myself in, hit one or two boundaries and then I decided to target that over. But I didn't start the over thinking that I was going to hit six sixes."

After coming down the track and hitting the first ball over long-on, Gibbs put the second and third sixes over long-off. Van Bunge then started to lose heart and bowled a full toss which was promptly thumped over mid-wicket for the fourth six.

"The straight boundaries were quite short so I targeted

them and hit him back over his head for six," recalls Gibbs. "On a normal-sized ground they would have been only fours so that was my bit of luck. I didn't have anything to lose because we had quite a few runs already at that stage so it didn't really matter whether I got out or not. After I'd hit three, I decided that I was going to keep on going and after the fourth one, I thought it could be on. I thought about using my feet and coming down the pitch but then I changed my mind and decided to stay in the crease."

With the last two balls, van Bunge tried to bowl a little shorter and Gibbs simply rocked back and pulled one six straight back over the bowler's head and then swatted the final one with a horizontal bat over mid-wicket.

"When I hit the fifth one," he says, "I didn't know what to do. I just had this huge grin on my face. Obviously, there was a delay before the last ball and that's when the thought hit home: 'maybe, this could be my day by hitting six in a row.' I stuck in the crease and he just bowled it in the slot again and I managed to hit it quite cleanly. It was probably the biggest one of the lot."

With another big grin on his face just visible through his helmet visor, Gibbs then walked down the wicket to exchange high fives with Kallis while his team-mates and the crowd celebrated wildly.

"When the last ball went over the boundary, I didn't actually know what to do," recalls Gibbs. "Should I do some star jumps or kiss my helmet or raise my bat? Having watched it a few times since, it's more the expressions and celebrations of the team that are beautiful to watch. I think they enjoyed it more than I did, it was just magnificent to see. I tried to hit some more sixes in the next over and I was caught."

Not only did his innings of 72 from 40 balls help South Africa to a very comfortable 221-run win, it led to the Habitat for Humanity housing charity receiving a welcome windfall of £515,000 – courtesy of the Johnnie Walker whisky maker. The tournament sponsors had promised to donate the sum when six sixes were scored for the first time.

"It's up there with the best things I've done," says Gibbs. "I never thought about getting six in a row but if it's your day, it's your day. I knew about Garry's record but I actually thought he had done it in a Test match so it was quite nice to be the first player to score six sixes in international cricket. That made it a bit more special and to do it in a World Cup was the icing on the cake."

For a time, Gibbs' innings appeared to have ended 24-year-old van Bunge's international career. The gifted all-rounder had scored a record 3,400 runs for MCC Young Cricketers in three seasons and hit their fastest hundred in just 38 balls against Surrey Under-19s in 2004. He also picked up the wickets of England batsmen Nick Knight, Michael Vaughan and Andrew Flintoff for 16 runs in a 2003 World Cup game. His initial response to being hit for six sixes was suitably phlegmatic.

"You could moan and groan and cry about it but the only way to deal with it is to have a little laugh about it," he said. "It's happened and I can't do anything about it. In fact, it was good hitting, it was quite nice."

"Before the game we said let's make history today by beating South Africa", said Dutch captain Luuk van Troost. "We made history, but not by beating them. What can you say? I told Daan after the third ball, 'try to bowl a quicker one' and he said, 'I just did'. There were a few good balls in it and a few shit ones. It's terrible to be a captain in that situation – I didn't know where to put my players anymore. It was a nightmare."

"I'm not too sure if I felt sympathy for Daan," says Gibbs, "but I did have a quiet word with him afterwards. We exchanged signed tops and on his he wrote 'they were only small sixes' which probably made him feel a little better."

But not enough to prevent van Bunge from announcing

his retirement from international cricket a month after the World Cup. He decided to concentrate on pursuing a career in sports management but would continue to play for Excelsior '20 Schiedam in the Dutch Hoofdklasse.

"The time has come when I have to choose," he said. "I've considered alternatives, such as only being available for home matches, but I have to give priority to my studies, and it wouldn't be fair to players who are fully committed to training and playing if I were to take a place in the side."

But in February 2008, van Bunge returned to the fold when he was included in the Netherlands squad to play against Namibia and the United Arab Emirates in the Intercontinental Cup.

Since that history-making over, Gibbs seems to have been treading water. He hasn't appeared in a Test match since January 2008 and although he played in a one-day series in Bangladesh, he was only first reserve for the South African tour of England this summer. His record in the shortest version of one-day cricket, Twenty20, has been disappointing – either with the Cape Cobras in South Africa, the Deccan Chargers, who finished bottom of the Indian Premier League, or Glamorgan.

The latest but probably not the last batsman to join the Six Sixes Club is Yuvraj Singh who, like Gibbs, made his own piece of history by achieving the feat for the first time in a game between two Test-playing nations on 19th September 2007. Again, it was during a World Cup but this time the competition was Twenty20. On his way to helping his country beat Pakistan in the final, the Indian all-rounder extracted revenge for being hit for five sixes in an over by England's Dimitri Mascarenhas in the NatWest Series at The Brit Oval a fortnight earlier. The unfortunate victim was Stuart Broad, the England and Nottinghamshire right-arm medium-fast bowler, who was targeted in the penultimate over. Umpire Billy Doctrove had just been forced to intervene after Yuvraj and Andrew Flintoff had become involved in an angry verbal exchange over an earlier boundary from a miscued hook off the Lancashire all-rounder. Under the floodlights of the Sahara Stadium at Kingsmead in Durban, Yuvraj hammered his way into the records books in front of a delirious crowd of nearly 16,000 – including *The Independent's* Stephen Brenkley:

"The manner of it was as remarkable as the statistical element, and from the third ball on there was an air of inevitability to it. If Broad lost his composure as the over wore on, it was entirely understandable. Yuvraj batted as a man who recognised he could put the ball anywhere. He was in what sportsmen like to call the second zone and the ball was being propelled into any zone he wished.

"The first ball went out of the ground over long-on, the second was flicked disdainfully over backward square leg, the third was smashed through extra cover as the batsman stepped away. The fourth, delivered from round the wicket, was a full toss which was dispatched to the backward point area, the fifth went to mid-wicket, and the sixth was more or less back where it started.

"Broad was searching for one simple yorker but it proved utterly elusive. Still, had he unleashed one, it was probable that Yuvraj would have nailed that too, so urgently was he moving round the crease."

The England captain, Paul Collingwood, summed it up succinctly as "the best striking I have ever seen. I have never seen hitting like it." Yuvraj reached his fifty in 12 balls as India made 218 for four and eventually won by 18 runs. He had scored the fastest international half-century of all time, beating Sanath Jayasuriya's 17-ball innings for Sri Lanka against Pakistan in Singapore in 1996.

"It was a horrible feeling for me at The Oval and Stuart is one of their main bowlers, so I feel sorry for him," Yuvraj said afterwards. "I had so many phone calls from people making fun of me, I thought 'God, that is not right, you have to give it back to me.' Tonight, he gave it back to me. Those words I exchanged with Flintoff spurred me on for sure. I wanted to give it back with the bat. We had wickets in hand so I thought, 'use the crease' and I timed the ball well. After the fourth one, I thought it was possible and I had to go for the next two."

"It was a poor over, and it got hit, but I didn't dwell on it," recalls Broad who, at the time, had yet to make his Test debut. "Fortunately, we went straight to Sri Lanka and I took wickets in every game to get it out of my system and I ended up as our second leading wicket-taker. Now, it couldn't be further from the back of my mind: those six balls didn't suddenly make me a bad bowler, and I can even laugh about it with people. It did hurt me at the time, but I'm the type of person who tries not to get too high when things go well so I don't get too down on myself when they go badly. It was pleasing to move on and get on with my career, without letting it eat away at me.

"Six sixes will happen more often. Batsmen have such a licence in Twenty20, they don't have to worry about being dismissed, the boundaries are often shorter so the scores are going up. When it started, 150 was a good total, now it's 200-220."

Yuvraj did not go unrewarded for his incredible innings. He was given a Porsche car and just over £125,000 by the Board of Control for Cricket in India. Six weeks later, he was inspired to make his highest Test score by hitting 169 off 203 balls in a drawn game against Pakistan in Bangalore. Like Gibbs, Yuvraj is a fine fielder and he led Kings X1 Punjabi to the semi-finals of the Indian Premier League in 2008.

By coincidence, Ravi Shastri, the second man to hit six sixes in 1985, was commentating at the time of Yuvraj's assault on Broad. As the newest and most exciting form of cricket continues to grow in popularity, the former all-rounder is aware, as a fellow Indian, of the impact that Yuvraj's innings will have on the player himself.

"Of all I have done in cricket, that over against Baroda is probably what people most remember," says Shastri. "Cricket is our national game and this will be a huge thing for Yuvraj. It was an amazing achievement by a fine player. That was some of the finest clean hitting I've seen in a long, long time. I knew that he was thinking only one thing: 'I've got nothing to lose here – let me go for it' and during the over, I described Stuart in commentary as having a 'scrambled brain' because I knew exactly what he was thinking. Where should I bowl? Should it be a yorker? Should it be off-stump or a short delivery down the leg-side? It's something he'll have to live with for the rest of his life – there's nothing he can do about it now – but Stuart has a very good temperament, he's young and talented so I'm sure he'll put that behind him and go on to play for England for some time. And I think a few more bowlers will be joining the Six Sixes Club – especially with the amount of Twenty20 and one-day cricket that's being played today."

FORTY YEARS ON

Garry Sobers is generally acknowledged to have been the greatest all-rounder ever to have played the game. But mention his name to most people, whether they follow cricket or not, and they will invariably make the connection with the six sixes. Sobers might not like it, and at times he is noticeably irritated by it, but as long as cricket is played throughout the world, the man and the moment will always be linked together. The six sixes represented a unique landmark in the history of the game and although the achievement has been equalled and emulated, it can never be beaten. Much as sometimes he might like to, Sobers will never be able to escape from the events of that August Bank Holiday Saturday at St Helen's in Swansea in 1968.

"I knew I had made history because nobody had hit six sixes before but it has never really ranked in my career," says Sobers. "People just love it because they've seen it on television and they always mention it to me. When I go anywhere, the first thing people ask me about is the six sixes. To a lot of them, it seems the only thing that I've ever done in my life is hit six sixes! People don't seem to realise that I did a little bit more than that in my career."

Sobers' attitude towards the worldwide attention created by his historic innings is understandable because he achieved so much else in the game but he well knows that the feat has played its part in enabling him to make a comfortable living on the after-dinner speaking circuit since he retired 35 years ago. It may be exasperating to have to re-visit the memory bank so often but people will pay good money to hear him talk about the six sixes as part of an overall review of his glorious career.

And it's not only cricket enthusiasts who have reserved a special place in their hearts for his ground-breaking innings.

The players are proud to have taken part in such a memorable event. The non-striker, John Parkin, his team-mates sitting up near the visitors' dressing room and the helpless Glamorgan fielders all have very fond memories of the day. As Sobers deservedly continues to be feted for his most famous feat, what have his former team-mates and their opponents been doing over the last 40 years and how do they look back on his achievement? A run-through the Glamorgan and Nottinghamshire batting orders would seem as good a way as any of finding out.

Alan Jones was a member of the Glamorgan side which, a year after the six sixes, won the county championship for the first time since 1948. Once again, he was his usual prolific self, scoring nearly 1,500 runs at an average of 42 to top the county's batting averages.

"Everything gelled," he recalls. "We'd had a couple of good years, coming second in 1963 and third in 1965 and 1968 and it was a case of everyone believing that we could win the championship after coming so close."

In 1970, Jones was picked to play for England against the Rest of the World in a five-match series following the last-minute cancellation of the planned tour by South Africa in the wake of the Basil D'Oliveira selection row. Sobers agreed to captain the Rest of the World side on condition that it was given Test status and Jones made his debut with fellow opener Brian Luckhurst. He scored five and nought and was caught behind twice by Farokh Engineer off Mike Procter. Although *Wisden* recorded that he "seemed overcome by the occasion", Jones denies that he froze on the big stage.

"It was all in the mind. I knew when I walked out of the pavilion at Lord's that I had to get runs or I'd be a forgotten man and that proved to be the case. I had scored lots of runs against Mike in country cricket but I simply had a bad day. Every player is entitled to a few of those ... my misfortune is that my bad game happened to coincide with the biggest match of my career. Unlike today, the selectors didn't say 'you're good enough to be selected for England – we're going to give you three Test matches to show what you can do'. The sad thing is that I know I was a much better player than I proved to be on that day and that's the hardest thing to take."

To add insult to injury, after being dropped, Jones then had his one cap struck from the record when the International Cricket Council decided in 1972 that official Test matches could only be between national sides. The one-cap wonder returned to being an uncapped opener who was considered by many people, both in and outside Wales, to be one of the finest batsmen never to have played for England.

"I was chuffed when I arrived at Lord's to be given my cap, the two sweaters, the blazer and the tie by our captain, Ray Illingworth, and I couldn't believe it when I heard about the ruling. To this day, I still haven't been told that I didn't actually play for England and I still have the cap, blazer and jumpers."

Despite the ruling, the match was listed in *Wisden* as late as 1979 and the original snub has recently been compounded by the inclusion of the 2005 tsunami match in Test records. Jones refused to allow his personal disappointment to affect his Glamorgan career. He carried on scoring a prodigious number of runs, led the county to the 1977 Gillette Cup Final when they lost to Middlesex by five wickets and made a career-best 204 not out against Hampshire at Basingstoke in 1980 at the age of 41 before calling it a day in 1983 to go into coaching. He has recently retired to take up golf seriously.

"I'm pleased that I was in the field on the day when Garry Sobers made history. I say to people that I remember him hitting the six sixes at Swansea and they say: 'Oh! You were watching it?' They don't realise that I was playing in the game."

Jones' opening partner during the 1969 championship-winning season was normally Roger Davis who took 30 catches to help Glamorgan lift the title as he developed into a loyal and reliable all-rounder. Three years after his fifth ball 'catch' at St Helen's, Davis was on the receiving end of another Malcolm Nash delivery – this time with near-fatal consequences. Under Peter Walker's guidance, Davis had turned into an excellent fielder and he prided himself on his ability to get close to a batsman.

"The whole skill of fielding at short leg is not the catching," he explains, "but first, getting out of the way or covering up and second, working out fairly early where the batsman is going to hit the ball. So you don't watch the bat but his body. I'd got to the situation where as the batsmen played a forward defensive, I was trying to catch the ball off the face of the bat and that was silly. I was even fielding at short leg in Sunday League games."

During Glamorgan's championship match against Warwickshire in Cardiff in 1971, Nash bowled an in-swinger to opening batsman Neal Abberley, who is now coaching at Edgbaston. He was particularly strong on the leg-side but with this ball, he shaped up to cover-drive because he thought it was going to go across him.

"I was thinking he was playing for the off drive," recalls Davis, "so I might have an inside edge if he mis-hit it and I'd catch it square. All of a sudden, it swung into him and Neal changed his mind. He middled it through square leg and it hit me on the way. I must have seen it because I'd turned my head and the ball hit me on the left-hand side of my head. Had it been a couple of millimetres to one side, I'd have been dead straightaway – the ball would have hit a vein."

As it was, Davis was knocked unconscious and started to twitch and turn blue after swallowing his tongue. If it hadn't been for the Pontypridd rugby club doctor, Colin Lewis, who, by chance, happened to be watching the game, then he would have died. Lewis ran on to the pitch, turned Davis on his back, pulled his tongue away from his windpipe and gave him the kiss of life.

"All I remember is waking up in the pavilion and then being in the ambulance and in the nearby St David's Hospital. I was conscious but I didn't realise I had a blood clot on my brain. They cracked my skull to get it out, I was in hospital for about a month, I lost my speech and my memory – everything really. I was home probably about three weeks after the operation and back on a cricket pitch five weeks after that. The doctor said I should never play again but I didn't take his advice because I wanted to prove him wrong. I tried to go back to fielding at short leg but Tony Lewis, the captain, wouldn't let me. He said he couldn't take the responsibility: 'I saw you nearly die once and it would be on my conscience if you got hit again.' So I fielded at slip instead most of the time."

In 1975, Davis had his best year for Glamorgan, scoring more than 1,200 runs, but his form fell away in the following season and he resigned after the club surprisingly only offered him a year-long contract. In the last 30 years, he has become a successful estate agent and was instrumental in bringing the former England coach, Duncan Fletcher, to Glamorgan in 1997 when the county won the championship again.

"I'm always going to be known as the guy who caught the fifth ball of the six sixes," Davis says, "and people are genuinely pleased to meet or speak to me because of that, which gives me a certain kind of fame. I don't know about dining out on it but I've been bought a few pints. I'm always remembered for it but, at the end of the day, I didn't catch it did I? I was deemed not to have caught it legally."

Majid Khan bounced back from what he considered a disappointing season in 1968 to play a crucial role in Glamorgan's championship win the following summer. He scored 1,300 runs, including 156 out of a total of 265 all out as Glamorgan won the title by beating Worcestershire by 147 runs in Cardiff.

"I was sleeping in the dressing room," Majid recalls.

"Peter Walker came to wake me up and said 'it's time to bat' so I batted. In everybody's life, a time comes when everything goes your way on a particular day. As in 1967 when I hit those five sixes off an over for Pakistan, everything went my way. It was my best innings for Glamorgan because it was on a very poor pitch. In those days, Sophia Gardens didn't have an even bounce. Some balls would shoot along the floor and others would just take off from a good length or just short of a good length. As my innings progressed, I became aware of how significant it could become. Everything fell into place: I would say I did nothing wrong and whatever I did came off. In fact, it was the best innings of my life and it won us the championship."

Majid had another good day at the crease in 1972 when he scored the fastest hundred of the season in 70 minutes against Warwickshire and he took over the Glamorgan captaincy from the next summer. As he readily admits, it was not a huge success as, following the retirements of Walker, Lewis, Don Shepherd and Ossie Wheatley, Glamorgan finished in the bottom half of the championship.

"I enjoyed being captain from 1973 to 1976 in the sense that it was a challenge," says Majid, "but it was a new side as many of the old guard had retired. The adjustment for the new players was very difficult what with the three-day game and then the Sunday League and one-day cricket. They were obviously not up to the standard of those who had gone. I left halfway through the 1976 season and it was a sad way to go. By that time, there was a lot of pressure on the committee and the players to do well in both formats. We were not performing well and, in their wisdom, the committee started shedding players who they thought weren't good enough or not performing to their potential. Some players became bitter, the whole atmosphere changed and the captain was the main figure so in the end I had to leave."

Majid retired from Test cricket in 1983 and became head of

sport with Pakistani Television where he stayed for the next 25 years. He was seconded to the job of chief executive of the Pakistan Cricket Board from 1996 until 1999, became an ICC referee and has also served on the ICC's cricket committee.

"I consider it to have been a privilege to be on the pitch that day and to stand next to Garry in the slips watching him," says Majid. "Regardless of who ever does it again, his name will stand as the first person to hit six sixes – just like Sir Edmund Hillary and Sherpa Tenzing Norgay will always be known as the first men to climb Everest. Others have conquered the mountain but their names will stand for ever – and so will Garry's."

After leading Glamorgan to only their second championship win in 1969, Tony Lewis' international career suddenly blossomed. He took an MCC team to Ceylon and the Far East in 1969-70 and three years later, after two potential skippers, Mike Smith and Ray Illingworth, had opted out of a tour to India, Pakistan and Sri Lanka, Lewis became the last man to captain England on Test debut – and one of a handful who have won their first game in charge. After scoring a first innings duck, he hit 70 not out in the second innings to guide England to their first win in India since 1951-52. Having made another eight Test appearances, an old knee injury from Lewis' rugby-playing days with Neath, Pontypool and Gloucester led to his retirement in 1974 and his career as a journalist and broadcaster, which had begun in the early 1960s, took centre stage.

"I wanted to be Neville Cardus and John Arlott rolled into one," he says. "They were the role models. Basically, I was always a writer and broadcaster who played cricket. I'd started writing for *The Sunday Telegraph* in 1963 and if I'd have been playing for my living, as Don Shepherd did, I'd probably have done better. At the same time, cricket was great fun and I really loved it. I was the paper's rugby and cricket correspondent until the Packer Circus arrived in 1977-78 when I gave up covering rugby and concentrated on cricket because there was so much."

After cutting his teeth as a rugby reporter with the BBC in Wales, Lewis later became a regular commentator on radio's *Test Match Special* and then fronted BBC Television's cricket coverage before retiring in 1991. He later became chairman of the Wales Tourist Board and then Welsh National Opera.

"I needed a change and the tourist board job suited my style of chairmanship because you needed to communicate and love your country. Then there was the 1999 Rugby World Cup which the board went big on and I then chaired the successful bid to bring the 2010 Ryder Cup to Wales for two years. It was a very competitive race – especially with Scotland."

Lewis has always maintained strong links with cricket. As well as writing the history of the MCC, he served as its president for two years and on numerous committees at Lord's and now, after recovering from two serious viruses, he is chairing the World Cricket Committee.

"I believe that MCC should be 'doing' things and not just 'being' things. We're still the custodian of the laws of the game and that's why we formed the World Cricket Committee which is more robust in its guardianship of the laws. We have the standing to make quite impartial statements and judgements because we're only concerned with cricket and cricketers. We can criticise the England and Wales Cricket Board or the ICC but we mainly try to complement their work.

"I always go back to the great writers on cricket, like C.L.R. James, Neville Cardus and John Arlott. They said that the game reflects the society in which we live and I think that's pretty faithful these days. It's a wonderful game and it's good to have continuity.

"I have never especially reflected on the six sixes and what it meant in the history of the game. I felt sorry for Malcolm because he's got a reputation which he doesn't deserve. He used to get out some of the best batsmen, like Geoff Boycott and Barry Richards, because he was a fine left-arm over-the-wicket bowler. The six sixes was just an astonishing event wasn't it? Looking back, it becomes greater by the hour. At the time, the significance of the achievement never occurred to me but I'm sure it did to everyone else."

Like Lewis, Peter Walker became a full-time broadcaster and journalist when his playing days ended in 1972 after Glamorgan's cricket committee offered him a match-only contract for the new season. He too had begun working for BBC Wales as a freelance while still with the county and, as a news reporter, had covered the Aberfan mining disaster in 1966. Walker later worked for the early evening magazine programme, *Nationwide,* and regularly presented sport on the BBC *Wales Today* programme as well being the front man for BBC2's coverage of the John Player Sunday League from 1973 into the early 1990s. After running his own film and video company for a decade, he became director of development for the Cricket Board of Wales in 1996.

"The board's aim was to foster and develop amateur cricket with particular emphasis placed on creating opportunities for schoolboys and girls," Walker recalls. "I was able to hit the ground running because the late Tom Cartwright, the former Warwickshire, Somerset, Glamorgan and England all-rounder had, for more than a decade, been the National Coach of the Welsh Cricket Association. He had done all the preliminary spadework and saved me from what would have been a massive task. If junior cricket in Wales is now in good shape, much of the credit for this belongs to Tom and in my three years as director, I believe I did increase awareness of the joys and benefits of supporting junior cricket in each of the 22 Welsh local authorities."

Having recovered from colon cancer in 1999, Walker is now working on a novel for an American publisher and trying to reduce his golf handicap.

"I feel it was a privilege to have played with and against Garry Sobers. I was surprised, but then not surprised, by what happened at St Helen's because if anybody was going to hit six sixes off an over, it would have been that bloke. If you bowled a ball to Garry and he blocked it, you felt you'd won that one. I understand the view that because Malcolm Nash was bowling spin and the boundaries were short perhaps it wasn't as great a feat as some people make out but all the shots, apart from the fifth, would probably have cleared a 75-yard boundary on most grounds. I can also understand why Garry sometimes get irritated when people think that's all he did in the game. In his private moments, he would probably agree that it was a fantastic achievement. Garry wasn't someone who dwelt on records like that – he was much more interested in what was running in the 3.30 at Haydock."

In the six sixes match, Eifion Jones' wicket was one of two taken by Sobers after the wicket-keeper had played his part in a 59-run partnership with Walker which helped Glamorgan avoid the follow-on. Jones took his good form into the championship-winning season, averaging nearly 33 with the bat and helping to dismiss 67 batsmen – nine more than his nearest rival. He was even more successful in 1970 when he picked up 79 championship victims in a record Glamorgan total of 94 – including a unique seven dismissals in one innings against Cambridge University. His form during that summer almost won him a place on the winter Ashes tour and he took more than 1,000 victims in every form of cricket during his 14 years behind the stumps for Glamorgan. He now lives quietly in retirement in Pontarddulais, near Swansea.

Tony Cordle has swapped singing *Delilah* at The Fountain Inn in Pontarddulais for belting out the Canadian national anthem before basketball matches in his adopted home in British Columbia. He emigrated with his late wife, Una, after 20 years as player and coach with Glamorgan, having taken more than 700 wickets – including a career-best nine for 49 at Colwyn Bay in 1969.

The county's first overseas fast bowler is semi-retired but his life is anything but quiet. He works at St Michael's University School, a private, co-educational, day and boarding school in Victoria, for students from kindergarten to pre-university level. As well as coaching football and cricket, he has managed the St Michael's snack shop, The Tuck Store, since 1985.

"We have more than 500 kids who have to be fed," says Cordle, "and I supervise the operation when they come in to eat and watch sport on the television. The children come from all over the world – from places like England, Wales, America and Germany but mainly from China and Japan because they seem to be the countries with all the money right now."

Cordle is still involved with cricket coaching, most recently with the Canadian women's team, but is now more well-known for his voice. From singing *O Canada* in the school assembly twice a week, he has progressed to being the warm-up act before basketball games at the University of Victoria.

"I've been singing at the university for 12 years after some of the students who graduated from our school went there to play basketball and asked me to come along. Singing the national anthem before games has become a huge thing. They had another singer but she couldn't always make it and when she couldn't, they'd play a recording. So I went along and I've been going ever since. I sing *O Canada* twice on a Friday and twice on Saturday before the men and women's basketball games and if schools from America are playing at the university, then I have to sing the *Star Spangled Banner* as well. Everyone seems to enjoy it and, if for some reason, I'm not there and they have to play the recorded version, people don't particularly like it – they want to hear me sing."

After undergoing prostate cancer surgery nearly three years ago, Cordle is well and enjoying life. His abiding memory of the six sixes is the last ball that helped Sobers to create history.

"Gary was swinging even before Malcolm let it go. The ball pitched half way down the wicket and Garry just wound up and smacked it. Malcolm was absolutely shell-shocked but things like that happen."

Off-spinner Brian Lewis will always have particularly special memories of the 1968 game against Nottinghamshire. Not only did he make his highest score for Glamorgan and hit Garry Sobers for six, but the match turned out to the last first-class game he started as a professional cricketer. By the end of that season, his career was effectively over after he had mysteriously lost his bowling action.

"Every September, we used to go to Claverley Cricket Club in Shropshire for a weekend," Lewis recalls. "It was a very pleasant weekend which we spent socialising and playing a couple of matches. In one of them, I came on to bowl as normal. There was nothing untoward but towards the end of the over – either the fourth or fifth ball – my action just sort of locked. It was like a warning sign. I just felt there was something wrong. I bowled another couple of overs and then I was off. The game ended and I didn't think any more of it. But when I turned up at the indoor school at Neath for pre-season nets in 1969, I just could not bowl. It was horrendous. I'd hit my head and the side netting with my arm, the ball would fly into the net and it would hit the floor – it was like a scatter gun. I'd never seen anything like it. I was 24 and I couldn't do anything about this bowling action. It was a bit like when golfers get the 'yips' when putting. I kept on trying because I had a contract for the 1969 season. I had to try and bowl – to find my way through it."

Although Glamorgan were sympathetic and sent Lewis to

Lord's in an attempt to solve the problem, he couldn't bowl at all during the 1969 season. He played his first and last Sunday League game against Middlesex at Lord's in late August in a 72-run defeat in which he didn't bowl and was run out for four. He was twelfth man in the championship clincher against Worcestershire in Cardiff a week later.

"Although I was a decent fielder, I think Tony Lewis picked me as a sort of gesture," says Lewis. "As a substitute fielder, I took two catches in the game – Basil D'Oliveira off Malcolm Nash in the first innings and Tom Graveney off Tony Cordle in the second. That game made up a little for the disappointment and frustration I felt. I went up to The Oval for the last game of the championship against Surrey which we drew to remain unbeaten for the season but it was a bit flat for me. I know it wasn't a physical problem. Our England fast bowler, Jeff Jones, finished at the same time through an elbow injury and if I'd have suffered from that, I'd have been happier. It was a complete and utter mystery and I still think about it. Was it temperament or tension? I don't know."

Having already served his apprenticeship as a carpenter, Lewis went back to his job in Port Talbot and played local club cricket in Maesteg until he retired two years ago. His bowling action improved but never completely returned and so his dream of carving out a career as a professional cricketer was stillborn.

"I kept thinking that one day it would come back, I was always hoping but it never did. I don't think it's something you can ever recover from. I found it difficult to accept but you do your best and life goes on. During the six sixes, I wasn't really aware that history was being made at the time until the fifth one when I understood what was happening. I was pleased and privileged to be involved but I don't think I would have been too pleased if Garry had done it to me!"

After a successful testimonial in 1968, no doubt helped by

his skippering of the Glamorgan team which beat Australia in Swansea, Don Shepherd continued to play for the county for another four years. As the wickets kept tumbling, the calls for him to be picked for England continued to fall on deaf ears. John Arlott, writing in Shepherd's testimonial brochure about his non-selection, summed up the situation perfectly:

"Few men have been so consistently penetrative without making a Test appearance. It is a little sad that he never had that opportunity."

After taking 69 championship wickets at just over 24 to help Glamorgan win the title in 1969, Shepherd did go on the tour to MCC team to Ceylon and the Far East in 1969-70 with team-mates Tony Lewis and Alan Jones but the elusive England cap remained just that.

"I never thought along the way that I was going to play," he says. "I never got up to have a look at the newspapers when the teams were going to be announced because I just didn't think it was going to happen. In fact, I've had more publicity and people know more about me because I didn't play for England. I don't think I ever lost any sleep over it but it would be nice to say I had now, because my two grandsons are playing for West Glamorgan and attending the Welsh nets."

Not everyone was unappreciative of Shepherd's bowling skills. His form in the championship-winning season led to him becoming one of the *Wisden* Cricketers of the Year in 1970 when he finished top of the national bowling averages after taking 101 wickets. Two years later, Shepherd retired after captaining the side in his last championship match against Surrey at The Oval after he had taken his 2,218th first-class cricket – although he did play in a couple of John Player League games before the season ended. After returning to run the family shop in Parkmill, Shepherd helped to coach the Glamorgan bowlers when Tony Lewis was club chairman and he has worked extensively as a pundit for BBC Wales television and radio over the years.

"Despite all my reservations about the way modern cricket is going – with the emphasis more on the one-day game than on county and Test matches and the fact that everything in bowling is sacrificed for pace – I'm still in love with the game, like an old fool. I can understand six sixes being scored twice last year because modern equipment, especially bats, is far superior and the players don't have to hit the ball that hard to get boundaries. The first time was special and I'm glad I was there because Garry was a guy who did so much for the game."

After having to leave the field with sore shins and not bowling again in the six sixes match, Ossie Wheatley recovered in time to turn in another impressive display as Glamorgan's season of promise ended with an innings defeat by Kent in their final game. His seven for 103 at Folkestone meant Wheatley finished with 82 wickets at 12.95. He topped the national bowling averages and was chosen as one of five *Wisden* Cricketers of the Year.

Having effectively retired, Wheatley was wheeled out once again for six championship games in the 1969 title-winning season and will always be remembered for his crucial contribution in Glamorgan's penultimate match against Essex at Swansea. Chasing 190, Essex needed three runs off the last ball to win. Roger Davis bowled it, John Lever dabbed the ball through gully down to the third man area and set off in pursuit of what looked like an easy two runs which would secure them a tie.

"Lever chopped it down almost intentionally to Wheatley at third man," reported *The South Wales Echo,* "as if realising that the Glamorgan player is weak on his fielding."

"I'd been put out in the deep where they thought I wouldn't be able to do too much damage," recalls Wheatley. "I had to run in a bit and as I did, I was saying to myself that I mustn't cock it up: I had to pick up the ball. I didn't practice fielding very much at that stage – I was too old and tired for that – so I really had to get it right. I had a chance to pick up the ball and line up the throw and, by a freak of nature, I threw it fairly straight, one bounce, to our wicket-keeper, Eifion Jones, who ran out Lever by a good three yards. John was unlucky because he thought that normally he would have got away with it. I remember it well as one of those odd sporting moments when somebody does something slightly out of character."

Wheatley finally did retire in 1970 to pursue his various business interests and a career in cricket and sports administration. He served as chairman of Glamorgan and The Sports Council for Wales and, as an England Test selector, he was closely involved with the notorious fall from grace of England skipper Mike Gatting in 1988 in the wake of his infamous spat with Pakistani umpire Shakoor Rana and the barmaid-in-the-hotel-bedroom affair. Wheatley has recently relinquished his role as chairman of The Cricket Foundation which runs The Chance to Shine scheme – the project aiming to bring cricket back to state schools – and he now owns a pub and some property in South Wales.

"I think it was highly apposite that it was Garry Sobers who hit the first six sixes. It would have been a pity if some slogger had done it. He hit the ball cleanly – and really properly. It was a fine bit of cricket to witness and be part of."

After scoring nearly 8,000 runs and taking more than 100 catches, Alan Rees started his last championship game for Glamorgan at Derby a fortnight before being summoned to St Helen's as the official substitute for the injured Wheatley in the match against Nottinghamshire. Between 1969 and 1971, he played half a dozen one-day games for the county, mainly in the John Player League, before securing a full-time job at the Afan Lido leisure centre, near Port Talbot, where he stayed until 1990. He then worked for a local car dealer before retiring in 1995.

"My sacking by Glamorgan in 1968 wasn't easy," he says.

"Although I always felt very upset, I tried not to show it. I didn't play cricket for money, I played because I had the daffodil on my chest. When the overseas players' rule was relaxed, Glamorgan's policy of having an all-Welsh team started to fall away. Majid came in, then the West Indian, Bryan Davis, and I think I was the scapegoat – it certainly didn't help my cause. Running Garry Sobers out for a duck at Cardiff in 1963 means more to me than being on the field at St Helen's because I took part in the first game. I didn't play any part in the six sixes: I was a spectator like the hundreds of other people who were in the ground."

Unlike Glamorgan, Nottinghamshire were unable to build on their successful season in 1968. Their fourth-place finish may have won Sobers his champagne bet and arrested their decline but the dramatic improvement proved only temporary. While Glamorgan finished first and third in the championship in the next two seasons, Nottinghamshire started to slip back down the table until reviving again in the late 1970s and 1980s.

Opening batsman Bob White's move to Nottinghamshire in 1966 proved the making of him as a cricketer. In eight years at Middlesex, he bowled fewer than a dozen overs and didn't take a wicket but when he retired in 1980 he had taken nearly 700 while at Trent Bridge. Encouraged by Sobers, he became a useful all-rounder in both first-class and one-day cricket. After retiring, White was appointed second-team captain and coach before leaving Trent Bridge under something of a cloud.

"Notts said they couldn't afford to keep me on anymore," he recalls. "It was either me or Ken Taylor, the then manager, who would be getting the sack. I wasn't very happy at the time but within a year I realised they'd done me a favour because I became a first-class umpire. I wanted to stay in the game and the powers that be at Lord's must have thought that as I'd been around for a few years, I must know what I was doing. I enjoyed umpiring until the last couple of years when there was a bit too much cheating. The players respect ex-players as umpires – they know you're going to make mistakes. I retired in 2001 so, after going on the ground staff at Lord's at the age of 16, I did 50 years in the game. Obviously, being part of the six sixes was a big highlight – it was a privilege to have been there and to have played with Garry."

Brian Bolus' 140 in the game against Glamorgan helped him to top the Nottinghamshire averages in 1968 after scoring more than 1,500 runs at an average of 38. He succeeded Sobers as captain in 1972 before becoming the third player to be capped by three counties when he moved to Derbyshire the following year. He retired from first-class cricket in 1975 to pursue a career in recreation and amenities in local government.

"I don't look back on my playing career with enormous pleasure," says Bolus. "I played county cricket for 20 years but my reflection is that I should have done much better than I did – although other people might have thought I didn't deserve to do as well as I did! Looking back on the six sixes, Garry was such an outstanding player, so far beyond, in my opinion, anyone playing in the game at the time. I think he's the greatest cricketer that's ever lived. He had always been so capable of the outrageous and the unbelievable that this was just another episode in the Sobers saga. He was a man of such monumental achievements throughout the whole of his career that this was just the next thing. While he was at Notts, Garry was an extraordinarily decent man and a wonderful ambassador for his race at a difficult time."

In 1994, Bolus became a Test selector and was chairman of the England Management Advisory Committee from 1998 to 2002. He served as Nottinghamshire's president in 2004 and 2005 and is now a vice-president.

"When I retired from local government, I genuinely felt that I'd never forgive myself if I didn't make a contribution at

Trent Bridge and maybe with England. I was elected a selector for a year and then did some scouting as a Test observer before being elected to EMAC and going on to serve as chairman for four years. I got the name changed to the International Teams Management Group just before I left. I didn't like the fact that it was too much of a committee and I believed we needed more involvement from the executives at Lord's. I felt more responsibility should be put on them. During my time, central contracts and the national academy came in but when I look back, I think I ought to have done more."

Graham Frost will always be grateful to Sobers for giving him the chance to bat up the order in his first season as a professional with Nottinghamshire in 1968. In his six years at Trent Bridge, he played more than 170 matches and has fond memories of the former West Indian captain whom he once ran out in a game against Gloucestershire at Newark in 1971.

"I opened and after a reasonable start, we were 77 for three when Garry came in at number five," recalls Frost. "He hit the ball to long-on when he was on six and I thought there was an easy two. I was halfway back for the second when I realised Garry was standing at the same end as me! I tried to get back but we'd crossed so he had to go. 'Don't worry about it son,' he said. 'These things happen – just go and get a hundred.'

"That's the type of guy he was – and I nearly did. I got 89 out of our total of 197, Garry top-scored with 86 when we batted again but we lost by nine wickets."

Under Sobers, Frost developed from being just a top-order batsman into an effective limited-overs bowler. His best figures of five for 33 came during a John Player League match against Worcestershire – again at Newark in 1971.

"I became a bits-and-pieces cricketer because Garry pushed me forward as a bowler. He threw the ball to me on a number of occasions in one-day cricket and despite my initial reservations, when The Great Man throws the ball to you, you've got to produce haven't you? I was second change and during my seven overs, I took the wickets of Ron Headley, Glenn Turner, Alan Ormrod, Norman Gifford and Brian Brain as Worcestershire made 202. I went in when we were 191 for four and Garry was going well. It was right towards the end, it was getting a bit tight and in the penultimate over, I hit a six straight over the pavilion and into the nearby cemetery. 'Brilliant!' said Garry. I think he then said something to the effect of 'you make it look so easy!' before going on to finish off the game with four balls left as he made 116."

Frost retired from the game in 1973 at the age of 26. He had picked up a few knee injuries, his contract wasn't being renewed and he decided to finish playing cricket and take up golf instead. After working as a newsagent for 16 years, he later ran two indoor cricket schools and now works as a courier. Five years ago, he was diagnosed with prostate cancer but was given the all-clear early in 2008.

"My one regret is that I didn't become an umpire," Frost reflects. "That was the biggest mistake I've made because I think I would have made a very good one – I'd have shot a few out! The six sixes are still vivid in my mind and I always tell a good story about it. My children have heard it that many times and it always comes up in conversation when we're at dinner and things like that. I will never forget that moment because it was the first time it had ever been done. Whatever part I played, though not as flamboyant as Garry's, I'm proud to have been in the team. Put it this way, I put in the groundwork for Garry to come in and hit the six sixes!"

After finishing as the championship's top wicket-keeper with 72 victims in 1968, Deryck Murray spent another season with Nottinghamshire and played for four years for Warwickshire in the 1970s. He retired in 1981 having won 62 caps for the West Indies. In 1992, he acted as referee in six one-day internationals and has been president of the

Trinidad and Tobago Cricket Board for the last three years.

"I have a very vivid memory of the six sixes over," Murray recalls. "It was unique. This was a genuine game where the bowlers and fielders were genuinely trying to get the batsmen out: it was a very special moment.

"Apart from being a colleague of Garry's, I'm a great fan of his so I just enjoyed watching what he was doing. Not many people can truthfully say they were there that Saturday. A lot of people say they were but I know there weren't 30,000 people in the ground. But I was and I was quite pleased that Malcolm Nash got his comeuppance after he'd bowled me with that dreadful ball in our first innings!"

Mike Smedley's 27 runs in Nottinghamshire's first innings against Glamorgan in the six sixes match may not have been the quickest of his career but he played a crucial part in the eventual victory at Swansea. In their second innings, Nottinghamshire had collapsed to seven for three but a solid 24 from Smedley, including a six off Malcolm Nash, pulled the situation around and allowed Sobers to set up a match-winning declaration. Smedley ended the season with more than 1,100 championship runs and retired in 1979 with an overall career average of 33.

In 1971, he was part of a rare hat-trick of hundreds involving the first three Nottinghamshire batsmen in a championship game against Sussex at Trent Bridge. It coincided with Ladbrokes' decision to open a betting office at Trent Bridge for the first time and although John Snow was on Test duty, Tony Greig, Mike Buss, John Spencer, Ken Suttle and Uday Joshi were part of the Sussex attack. Mike Harris and Graham Frost put on 170 for the first wicket before Frost was dismissed for 104. Smedley replaced him and put on another 170 with Harris who was the next man out for 141.

"It's not unique to have numbers one, two and three scoring tons but it doesn't happen very often," says Smedley.

"It was a good day for batting and the two partnerships made it a lot easier. At the fall of each wicket, there was a march by supporters towards the betting booth underneath the scoreboard and with the way I was playing after tea, a lot of people had put money on me to be the highest scorer. They were a bit disappointed that Brian Bolus took some of the bowling when he replaced Mike so they booed him because he was blocking later on. He finished on 25 not out and I had 131 not out and Garry declared on 416 for two the next day."

"That century was my highest score of the season," recalls Frost. "Guess what I made in the second innings? A duck – but that sums up cricket!"

Smedley has recently retired from working for a portable heating and air conditioning company and spent seven years running a newsagents in the 1980s.

"I do think about the six sixes match from time to time," he admits. "I'm not surprised it's only been done three times since because it's such a difficult thing to do. Garry's achievement was outstanding. In a practice game, I once hit six fours in an over. It was fantastic being part of a match where history was made. It's down in the record books isn't it? When people look at the scorebook, they'll see me down as the last man out."

And they will also see that John Parkin was the other not out batsman. Forty years later, the man whose name has become the answer to one of the most famous pub quiz questions of all time remembers the six sixes well – and especially a conversation he had in his hotel room the next morning.

"I answered the phone and it sounded like a proper call from a newspaper reporter," recalls Parkin. "He said he wanted to talk to me about my part in the six sixes but I said I couldn't. It took me a couple of minutes to realise that it was a spoof call. It was Deryck Murray winding me up – I'd heard some of the other players giggling in the background!"

The Glamorgan match turned out to be Parkin's last first-team championship game for Nottinghamshire. In 1969, he returned to the seconds before being told that his contract would not be renewed for the new season.

"In a way, I was relieved because I had been thinking about packing it in anyway," he says. "I hadn't enjoyed it at all. In my own mind, I wasn't quite good enough. People thought I could have made it and when I went back to captain the second team in 1972, I was a different player altogether because the onus was taken off me. We had some good youngsters like Derek Randall and Dusty Hare, the former England rugby full-back, I batted at seven or eight and it didn't matter whether I scored any runs or not. I could go in and score runs freely and, more often than not, when I was asked to do it, I did it. We won the second X1 championship in 1972 with young lads like Paul Todd, Philip Wilkinson, Nirmal Nanan, and Derek, who you could see was going to be an England player. He was with us for only half a season and then he got into the first team. I remember scoring 49 against Leicestershire at Loughborough in 1972 when Derek hit 100 not out off 102 balls – his talent stood out."

While he was captaining the seconds for three years, Parkin worked as a milkman and also skippered his local village team, Kimberley, for a very successful decade. He has recently retired after spending nearly 30 years as a bricklayer. Every now and then, the six sixes and his fleeting brush with fame crop up in conversation.

"A few of the local lads have come up to me and said 'I've had a drink on you!' They've got talking to somebody involved in cricket and they've asked them the question: 'I bet you a pint you don't know who the other batsman was when Garry Sobers hit the six sixes?" That's a nice way to be remembered. The one thing I'll never forget about that day is thinking about backing up, wanting to get down the other end and getting ready to run. In many ways, it sums up my position as a cricketer. I never felt that I was quite as good as my team-mates and there I was, a solid and reliable cricketer basically just holding up my end while Garry Sobers, a brilliant player, was making history. I was closer to the action than most people but I wasn't doing any more than anyone else. Any of our three remaining batsmen could have been stood there. To be quite honest, I've always been embarrassed by it.

"My kids, Lynne and Claire, have seen the footage and they fall about laughing because I had hair then. A few years ago, Garry signed a copy of his autobiography for my wife, Joyce, in Nottingham and she presented it to me when I came home from work. I'm proud to have been part of a world record and that piece of history is going to be there forever isn't it?"

As Sobers was hitting Malcolm Nash around St Helen's, Richard Bielby was waiting to come in to bat. He had joined Nottinghamshire in 1967 and played 43 games for the county before retiring in 1971. He then became involved in selling computer games and now lives in retirement in France.

Medium-fast bowler Mike Taylor won't ever forget the six sixes game. After taking two wickets in Glamorgan's first innings, he later became the match-winner on a rain-affected pitch by taking five for 47 but was denied the opportunity of reaching an important milestone by the skill of a team-mate. Chasing 280 runs to win in 248 minutes, Glamorgan had subsided to 113 for nine leaving Taylor tantalisingly stranded on 99 wickets for the season.

"Bob White was bowling from the other end at the death," Taylor recalls. "Ossie Wheatley and Don Shepherd were the last men in and my five wickets meant I needed one more to reach my hundred. Bob bowled five off-breaks at Don and then an arm ball which knocked his off stump out of the ground and they were all out! It was our last game and that was the nearest I ever came to reaching the magical 100 wickets in a season in my career. Mind you, I'll take 99 any time!"

From 1973 to 1980, Taylor played for Hampshire and he stayed with the county in an administrative capacity until retiring as assistant secretary and marketing manager in 2002.

"In terms of the six sixes, I was pleased to be in the right place at the right time. Garry had already scored the fastest hundred of the season at Dover and our attitude was: 'what else can he do?' And then, in the very last game of the season, he showed us – by hitting the six sixes!"

The last two members of the Nottinghamshire side who played against Glamorgan in 1968 have both died. David Halfyard, who had berated Sobers for declaring too early after the six sixes, took three wickets for 71 runs in the first innings and conceded 29 runs from seven overs in the second. He didn't bat in either Nottinghamshire innings.

"Dave came to us from Kent where he'd had his most productive years," recalls Brian Bolus. "He was a bit of a slogger with the bat, pretty slow in the field but a tremendous trier with the ball. He bowled seamers and in between times, a few leg breaks; he was a very effective performer."

During the 1968 season, Halfyard took 68 championship wickets and made what Taylor describes as some "miraculous recoveries" from injury. On the last day of a three-wicket win over Derbyshire at Trent Bridge in the middle of June, Halfyard pulled up in his delivery stride, took his sweater from the umpire and went off the field. He wasn't expected to play in the next day's Gillette Cup game at Worcestershire but, after a spell in the nets at New Road, he surprisingly declared himself fit and was picked.

"He had obviously pulled a muscle the day before," says Taylor, "so nobody believed that he could be fit. We made 226 off our 60 overs – with Garry hitting 95 not out – and then bowled them out for 178 with Dave conceding just 18 runs from his 12 overs of leg-cutters off three or four paces. It was incredible – he was quite a character."

Halfyard stayed for three years at Trent Bridge, taking his total of first-class wickets to 963, before spending the next 12 years playing for Durham, Northumberland and Cornwall, travelling around in a camper van. He later returned for a second spell as an umpire. When he died suddenly in 1996 at the age of 65, *Wisden's* obituary described his career as "remarkable, indeed eccentric... his pride and joy was a camper van with almost 400,000 miles on the clock; his cricket had the same improbable durability."

Barry Stead, who used to open the bowling with Sobers, had a quiet match at St Helen's, picking up a wicket in each of Glamorgan's innings. After taking seven for 76 against the touring Indians on his debut for his native Yorkshire in 1959, he had played for the Combined Services before joining Nottinghamshire in 1962. He spent 14 years at Trent Bridge and was the Professional Cricketers' Association's player of the year in 1974. Stead died from cancer in 1980, aged 40. *Wisden Cricket Monthly* described his "frantic, scuttling approach to the crease" as "one of the most riveting sights in county cricket."

"Barry was quite similar to another left-arm fast-medium bowler, Ryan Sidebottom, who plays for Nottinghamshire now," says Bolus. "When the wicket was a little green, we used to say to Barry: 'Just the wicket for a five foot eight left-arm swing bowler today Steady!' He was a genuine cricketer who always gave his best."

In 1972, Stead returned a career-best eight for 44 against Somerset, including a hat-trick, as he ended the season with 93 wickets at just over 20. When the Clive Rice-Richard Hadlee era began to dawn at Trent Bridge, a slightly slower Stead left to play some league cricket but was recalled by Nottinghamshire because of an injury crisis in 1978. He had the misfortune to drop a difficult, lofted catch from Lancashire's Jack Simmons which decided a John Player League match being shown live on BBC Television. Although obviously embarrassed, Stead managed his usual wide, ruddy and toothy grin.

So much then for the players but what about the bat and ball? What happened to them? The short-handled Slazenger bat was sold at auction by Christie's in Melbourne for just over £54,000 in October 2000 when a mystery telephone bidder paid nearly £10,000 more than the expected sale price. In the same lot, the bat used by Sobers when he hit the then record Test score of 365 fetched nearly £48,000.

For most of the last 40 years, mystery has surrounded the whereabouts of the ball used in the famous over. Various rumours have suggested that more than one ball was used, one of the sixes landed in a passing carriage of the Mumbles light railway (even though that stopped running in 1960) and the ball had been stolen from the museum at Nottinghamshire's ground.

The formal return of the ball by the Pontardawe schoolboy, Richard Lewis, to Garry Sobers took place at St Helen's on the morning of Monday 2nd September 1968 and was covered in the local and national press. All the papers reported that the ball's new home would be the museum at Trent Bridge with Pat Gibson revealing in that day's *Nottingham Guardian Journal*, that once he knew the ball was being returned to St Helen's, "Nottinghamshire scorer Arthur Wheat immediately claimed possession and it will be on its way to Nottingham tonight."

But according to Nottinghamshire's archivist and librarian, Peter Wynne-Thomas, the Test match ground didn't contain a museum in 1968.

"There were two glass cases in the Long Room and they held mainly 19th century memorabilia. When we started the library in 1978, they were dismantled and I saved the contents until we did get a bit of a museum in the 1980s. We had quite a number of cricket balls but they were almost all pre-1914 ones, with a connection with Alfred Shaw, John Gunn and Tom Wass and so on, but there were certainly no post-war ones. I don't ever recall the Sobers ball being in the Long Room. I have never seen the ball.

"The story of the six sixes has come up time and time again and various journalists have phoned me up about it over the years – presuming the ball is in the museum. I told them I knew nothing about it but, as a result, I did speak to members of the family of Arthur Wheat who died in the 1970s. His widow said she had never seen the ball at home so it never seems to have been in the Wheat household."

The alternative story to the one involving the museum is that the ball was given to the then secretary of the Nottinghamshire Supporters Association, John Gough, and kept in the Eddie Marshall Bar at Trent Bridge. Marshall was chairman of the association which was based in the bar. From there, the ball passed into the hands of Gough's successor, Josie Miller, who kept it in her make-up drawer until she decided to sell it two years ago.

"I suppose the simplest answer to it all is that Arthur Wheat brought the ball back to Trent Bridge and gave it to somebody in the Notts Supporters Association," says Wynne-Thomas.

In 2006, the ball was passed to Christie's in London, via Garry Sobers' agent, Basharat Hassan, a former Nottinghamshire player who now runs an events promotion company. Wynne-Thomas and his counterpart at Glamorgan, Dr. Andrew Hignell, discussed the intended sale on the telephone. Hignell travelled to London to verify the details of the match and was shown the ball.

At the auction in November, the ball was described as a "red leather Special County cricket ball, manufactured by Duke & Son, Nottingham, signed 'G. Sobers' (seam stained, quarter seam split, general scuff marks); with a certificate of provenance signed by Sir Garfield Sobers, stating 'that this signed cricket ball was bowled during the over in which I [Sobers] hit six sixes off Malcolm Nash."

According to Christies, three separate balls were used in the over, the first two being hit into the crowd and reportedly returned to the umpires. The third ball was used for the rest of the over before being hit out of the ground and then found by a "keen-eyed youngster" in St Helen's Avenue. The auctioneers had put a guide price of between £5,000 and £8,000 on the ball which was bought by an anonymous bidder for £26,400. A spokesman for the auction house said the price reflected the unique place the ball had in cricketing history. "We are thrilled that such a historic relic from the game of cricket was so sought after," he said.

When news of the sale reached Wales, doubts began to be cast on the ball's authenticity and *The Independent on Sunday's* Andrew Tong reported on the resultant disquiet among Glamorgan players. His article – headlined 'Howzat for a mystery: is this the most famous ball in cricket?' – pointed out that the ball sold at Christie's was made by Duke & Son of Nottingham but in 1968, Glamorgan only used balls made by Stuart Surridge, the cricket equipment company set up by the former Surrey player, which supplied balls to a sports shop just down the road from St Helen's.

"I think the authenticity of the ball sold at Christie's is questionable," says all-rounder Peter Walker. "The only person who can say with any authority whether that ball is the right one is the bowler, Malcolm Nash."

"I was really surprised when Peter called to tell me about the ball in 2006," says Nash. "I thought it was in the museum at Trent Bridge but I then heard it had been stolen or mislaid. When we were playing at home, either Tony Cordle, our other opening bowler, or I would go into the umpires' room and select the balls that we'd prefer to bowl with. All balls, however they're made, feel a little different. The team went along with my gut instinct of what I felt was good. Tony liked the ones that smelt really rich and the darker-coloured ones because he said they swung more. It's a fact that the ball we used on that day was a Stuart Surridge ball because Glamorgan never used anything else for home games. There have been various debates and arguments about whether it was changed – I can assure you it wasn't. We used the same ball all the way through the over. If you look at the BBC Wales footage you can see it coming back after every six. It wasn't changed and I should know because I was the one who had to let it go each time and then watch it disappear."

"Only one ball was used during the over," confirms Cordle. "I thought it was strange that a Duke & Co of Nottingham ball was involved because we always used Stuart Surridge ones. The only time we didn't was when we experimented with the Kookaburra from Australia for just one season when all the balls seemed to be going out of shape. It was thought they were a bad batch but it was probably because the bats became much bigger and heavier. We used Stuart Surridge balls because the Glamorgan scorer, Bill Edwards, had a contract with the firm to supply his sports shop with balls. It wasn't just in Swansea but whenever we played a game at home: even when we went to Colwyn Bay in North Wales, we always used a Stuart Surridge ball."

In the 1969 Glamorgan Members Newsletter, a review of the previous season contained a report on the meeting between Richard Lewis and Garry Sobers when the ball used in the over was taken back to St Helen's. Under a photograph of the two men with Glamorgan secretary Wilf Wooller, the over was reviewed and the story of the ball's discovery was briefly told. The report stated:

"Glamorgan presented this ball, which was made at the firm of Stuart Surridge, the former Surrey captain, to Nottingham to reside in a place of honour in their Sporting Museum."

The replacement ball given to Richard Lewis for returning the original one to Glamorgan now has pride of place in his home. It was made by Stuart Surridge.

KINDRED SPIRITS

Five minutes in Swansea have linked the names of Sobers and Nash together for all time in the record books. They were two cricketers with very different careers – one the greatest all-rounder of the modern age, the other a journeyman professional who never played for his country – but they shared the same characteristic of supreme self-belief and they both played the game in a positive spirit. With either bat or ball, Sobers and Nash liked to attack and were prepared to take risks along the way.

"I think people like to see attacking cricket," says Sobers, "They don't really enjoy watching the ball being blocked all the time. They want batsmen to hit the ball and I suppose six sixes in one over is the ultimate. But I never played cricket for records. I always went out to enjoy myself and try to win if possible and the records created were just one of those things."

"I had the same ideals, if not the same talent, as Garry," Nash says. "If you didn't attack people, you had no chance of getting them out. I had a burning ambition to prove myself, and the bigger the name I was bowling to, the bigger my desire to prove I had a right to be on the same field. I tried to get a batsman out with every ball I bowled."

Sobers' love of gambling is well-known and the West Indian captain would occasionally display his adventurous streak on the cricket field, sometimes with rather embarrassing consequences. Just six weeks before his first game for Nottinghamshire in 1968, Sobers made a declaration that infamously backfired in the fourth Test against England at Port of Spain after the first three games of the series had been drawn.

England had made 404 in reply to the home side's 526 for seven declared so the West Indies had a first-innings lead of

122. But when their second innings had reached 92 for two, Sobers suddenly jumped to his feet and waved his batsmen in. It was a brave decision. England needed 215 to win in 165 minutes and although initially reluctant to try to win the game, captain Colin Cowdrey led from the front with 71 and Geoff Boycott made 80 not out as the tourists won by seven wickets. Paceman Charlie Griffith had pulled a thigh muscle so couldn't bowl and the pitch did play better than expected but Sobers was slated for making what was considered to be a foolish and too generous declaration. The next day, when the teams arrived in Georgetown for the fifth Test, he had to be given a police escort. Despite the controversy as England went on to win the series 1-0, Sobers has remained unrepentant.

"I made that declaration for cricket," he says. "If I had not done so the game would have died. This way, the West Indies could have won. England had never scored at 40 runs an hour during the tour and I did not expect them to do so then.

"What I most remember is that we bowled at about 21 overs per hour throughout the innings and if we had bowled at 18, which would have been above average for Test cricket and much quicker than England's rate, even when they employed their spinners, we could easily have drawn the game. That never entered my mind. I was trying to win."

Sobers never deviated from that philosophy for the remaining six years of his career and he continued to make one or two over-generous declarations. Sadly for Nottinghamshire and their supporters, the county saw the best of him during his debut season of 1968 when he turned around the club by taking them to a remarkable fourth place in the table.

"That first season," he recalls, "I played in 26 matches in the championship, I scored more than 1,500 runs and bowled 773 overs and took 83 wickets – it was a satisfactory start."

But a combination of a deteriorating knee injury and his international commitments meant that Sobers didn't complete another full season at Trent Bridge until 1971. In that season, Nottinghamshire won only one of their first 16 championship games, were knocked out in the first round of the Gillette Cup and lost eight consecutive Sunday League matches. Sobers averaged 46, took 53 wickets and held 29 catches as they finished 12th in the championship. An operation on his knee meant he missed almost the whole of the 1972 season and he played just 15 championship games in each of his last two seasons at Trent Bridge.

But on the world stage, Sobers continued to confirm his position as the game's greatest player. He considers his best innings for the West Indies to be the undefeated 163 he hit in the second Test against England at Lord's in 1966 when he put on an unbroken 274 for the sixth wicket with his cousin, David Holford, to save the match. But his performance for the Rest of the World against Australia in Melbourne in 1972 is mentioned in the same breath – not least because of the comments of the legendary Australian batsman, Don Bradman.

The five-match series replaced the cancelled South African tour in the wake of the continuing controversy over apartheid. Sobers had been caught first ball off fast bowler Dennis Lillee in the first innings and in retaliation, when Australia batted, he bounced Lillee with his first ball and dismissed him with his second. In the Rest of the World's second innings, the score was 146 for three when Sobers came to the wicket. He drove Lillee's first ball for four and took 29 off his first three overs on his way to a hundred from only 129 balls. He eventually scored 254, Lillee finished with three for 133 off 30 overs and the Rest won by 96 runs.

Sobers himself says the innings was "probably as near to perfection as I ever came with the bat" while Bradman described it as "probably the best ever seen in Australia. The people who saw Sobers have enjoyed one of the historic events in cricket. They were privileged to have such an experience."

"Coming from Sir Donald, it was a great honour," says

Sobers. "because he had seen so many of the great players. The important thing about that innings was that when I was walking off, and they were all clapping, Dennis looked at me and said, 'I've heard about you and now I've got my tail cut properly.' Since then, Dennis and I have been the best friends that you could ever see."

Sobers played his first and last one-day international in 1973 when the West Indies lost by one wicket to England at Headingley and bowed out of Test cricket after a 26-run defeat by England in Port of Spain in 1974. His record speaks for itself: in 93 Tests for the West Indies, he scored 8,032 runs, including 26 hundreds, at an average of nearly 58 and took 235 wickets at 34 each, as well as 109 catches. He held the world record for the highest Test score after hitting 365 against Pakistan in 1958 until another West Indian, Brian Lara, made 375 against England 36 years later.

Every team Sobers played for, in England, Australia or the West Indies, was enhanced by his presence; everything he did was done with the greatest of ease. Cricket has produced several superb all-rounders, both before he started to dominate the game and after he had retired, yet Sobers is still considered to be the best of them all.

He was knighted in 1975 and made a National Hero of Barbados by Prime Minister Owen Arthur in 1998. In 2000, Sobers was named by a panel of experts as one of the five *Wisden* Cricketers of the Century when he received 90 votes out of a possible 100. The other four players selected were Don Bradman (100), Jack Hobbs (30), Shane Warne (27) and Viv Richards (25). Since retiring, Sobers has travelled the world promoting Barbadian tourism as well as serving as one of the ICC's international ambassadors. He is also a very popular speaker on the after-dinner circuit.

When Malcolm Nash retired, John Arlott, writing in *Wisden Cricket Monthly,* described him as a "thoughtful and sensitive cricketer" who was "never a bowler to settle for the slavishly defensive but sought to attack and to outwit opposing batsmen. He is, as he ruefully accepts, best known for being hit for six sixes in a six-ball over by Garfield Sobers in 1968."

Over the last 40 years, Nash has often been cast in the role of unfortunate victim but it would be unfair and disrespectful to dismiss his remaining 15 years in the game simply because he has an unenviable place in the record books. In fact, it could be argued that his career blossomed after the mauling he received from Sobers. What effect does he think the six sixes over has had on him?

"Zero. All it has done is create conversation – it's provided a public forum for debate and discussion. I had two options: I could either crumble and not play again or I could put it down as just another day in my life, another over to put behind me, and move on – which is what I did. It didn't knock my confidence or make me doubt my ability at all.

"I suddenly attained celebrity status. I went on talk shows with Garry and appeared as a guest on his *This is Your Life* programme. There is never a day goes by when people don't want to talk to me about it. I have never been uncomfortable about it. They were six balls in my life. It never bothered me one little bit and it still doesn't."

Nash remains unrepentant about his adventurous approach to bowling what turned out to be the last over of Nottinghamshire's first innings. Although some might consider his attitude a shade reckless or foolhardy, Superman stands by the way he tried to dismiss cricket's version of the comic book hero:

"I was never tempted to bowl a wide or a no-ball during that over because of the way I approached the game," says Nash. "It depends on your character but I think that experience made me stronger as a person, even thought I didn't bowl spin again for a long time!"

Nash won his county cap during the following season when Glamorgan lifted the championship, taking 71 wickets at nearly 19 and by the time he retired from the first-class game, he had amassed an impressive total of 993 wickets without ever taking 100 in any season. The South African opening batsman, Barry Richards, regarded Nash as one of the most difficult bowlers to hit and his fast-medium swing bowling earned him a Test trial in 1976 when he played for The Rest against England in Bristol. The night before the game, along with the two other opening bowlers, Chris Old and Alan Ward, he met with the captain, Mike Brearley, who told Nash and Ward they would be taking the new ball. The next day, Nash immediately repaid his skipper's faith by having Dennis Amiss caught off the first ball of the match before later picking up David Steele's wicket to finish with figures of 28-6-65-2.

"I thought I had a reasonable chance of being picked for England," Nash says. "It was the flattest of wickets and the ball didn't get up above knee-high. At the end of the first innings, Alec Bedser, the chairman of selectors and the England captain, Tony Greig, took me aside and suggested I should try to bowl a bit quicker – then I might play for England. I explained that people like the former Test bowlers, Wes Hall and Fred Trueman, had told me I would lose my swing if I bowled quicker. Bedser and Greig then talked about the need for someone to knock over nine, ten and jack and I said I was not a specialist quick bowler but a swing bowler – and there was a difference. The matter was never discussed further and I wasn't picked for England. Perhaps I was too honest for my own good but my strength was that I kept knocking over the first five batsmen with the new ball."

Nash also performed well in Sunday League games for Glamorgan and still holds their record for the most economical spells, returning figures of 8-4-8-1 and 8-4-8-2 against Lancashire in 1973 and 1980.

But lightning almost struck twice when he was hit for five sixes and a four in an over by Lancashire's Frank Hayes in

1977, again at St Helen's. This time, Nash was bowling his normal seam-up with the second new ball from the Mumbles Road End of the ground as Hayes made 119 in Lancashire's first innings.

"Frank was a good player," recalls Nash, "but his mistake was that he hit the second ball of the over for four after hitting the first one for six! What was going through my mind at the time? Thank God he hit the second one for four!"

Four days after that narrow escape, one of the biggest disappointments of Nash's career took place at the head-quarters of cricket. Under Alan Jones, Glamorgan had reached the final of the Gillette Cup against Middlesex who won the toss and elected to field. Glamorgan made only 177 but then Nash had opener Mike Brearley caught by Eifion Jones off the first ball of Middlesex's reply.

"Clive Radley came in and I thought I had him very early on when a chance went straight to Collis King at second slip," says Nash. "But he dropped it! Clive went on to make 85 not out and win the match. That's the only time in my career that I blamed someone for dropping a catch. I didn't blame Roger Davis for the fifth six against Garry Sobers but Collis' mistake was criminal. The ball came to him knee-high and he shelled it. If he hadn't who knows what might have happened?"

Nash was no mug with the bat himself. He hit a century before lunch off just 61 balls against Surrey at The Oval in 1976 on his way to his highest first-class score of 130. Surrey had made 338 and the Glamorgan wickets were tumbling as England bowler, Robin Jackman, worked his way through the top and middle orders. Nash was sleeping off a late night in the dressing room when he was told he was next man in. He joined Mike Llewellyn at the crease at 65 for six.

"I played and missed the first four balls," he recalls, "and Mike came down the wicket and reminded me that we were in a bit of a hole. 'I've had four sightings,' I replied. 'I'll take care of the situation.' And I did because I was seeing the ball like a pumpkin. When I got going, it was very exciting. I was 119 not out at lunch and that was probably the best knock of my career. Mike and I put on 161 for the seventh wicket as we made 271 all out and we eventually managed to hang on for a draw."

Two years later, Nash came close to putting himself in the record books alongside Sobers when he hit successive sixes off the first four balls of an over by Somerset spinner Dennis Breakwell at Taunton. It was a rare chance for him to create his own version of the six sixes.

"After the first two," he recalls, "their wicket-keeper, Derek Taylor, asked me what was going on. 'Watch this!' I said – and hit two more sixes.

"He then asked me if I was going to go for it. 'What do you think?' I said. But the last two balls were fired down the leg side. Obviously, Dennis didn't want to get me out."

"They were not huge sixes," wrote Alan Gibson in *The Times*, "but the fieldsmen never had any chance of catching them. This was a piquant situation, for reasons which cricketers know; but Nash could not manage to clobber two more sixes, as Sobers once did from him. Breakwell looked ruminative, but he had no reason to be depressed, for he had a good match."

For the record, Breakwell finished with three for 68 from 26 overs – after hitting 50 not out in Somerset's first innings – Nash scored 55 and Somerset won by nine wickets.

After captaining Glamorgan in 1980 and 1981, when they finished 13th and 14th in the championship, Nash retired in 1983 and then spent two seasons with Minor Counties side Shropshire. After a variety of jobs, he became involved with sports marketing which took him to Canada in 1991. He has since been a cricket coach, first in British Columbia and then with the United States Junior Cricket organisation in Kansas and California.

"I helped to organise the first Under-13 game between the USA and Canada in 2000 and Garry was our guest of honour. He was an ambassador of cricket for the ICC and this game was very much part of what we were doing with the development of junior cricket to get some profile. We had three one-day internationals in four days of cricket, it was absolutely fabulous and the kids had a blast – they thoroughly enjoyed it.

"Garry and I meet up when he comes to the States. We have a game of golf or go for dinner and he's been to the Philadelphia Cricket Festival, which is staged every May, as a special celebrity guest. Occasionally, somebody will put on a function where they want Garry, and thus me, to be there but we talk about other things now. The six sixes is a dead issue with us. We've moved on from that."

Nash is less involved with United States Junior Cricket these days and currently works in the sales department of a company specializing in urban landscaping in San Rafael, near San Francisco, where he now lives with his second wife, Nhon.

Forty years after the event which changed the lives of both Sobers and Nash, the memories may have faded a little but its impact has not diminished. It was a defining moment in the game. The rubicon had been crossed. It showed that it was possible for a cricketer in a first-class match to hit every ball of a six-ball over for six. Ted Alletson, 'Big Jim' Smith, Cyril Smart, Arthur Wellard and Majid Khan had all come close but the perfect set had eluded them all. In 1968, Sobers managed to pull it off. The names of the bowlers who suffered at the hands of Alletson and Co have largely been forgotten. That Malcolm Nash's remains is partly because the event was captured by the television cameras – the six sixes are one of the most viewed video clips on the YouTube internet site – and partly because the two men are joined at the hip through an event that made history.

"It was one of those days," reflects Sobers, "and one of those things. A lot of people don't realise that Malcolm was a good bowler. I think he had been on the verge of the

England team – not for his slow left-arm but his swing stuff. He was a very good swing bowler and a reasonably good spin bowler. I took chances and they came off and Malcolm thought at the time that he could get me out – and he nearly did. He was bowling to try to get me out which is the only thing you can do in cricket.

"Hitting six sixes was never on my mind at any stage until I faced that last ball because it virtually seemed impossible. When you consider that cricket had been played for so long before I started playing and the feat was never done, I can't see how I could think that I was going to do it. I think I was lucky to get it. It seems to have revolutionised cricket because it's been talked about all over the world – even in countries that know nothing about the game. Although I know kids love to hit the ball in the air and out of the ground, I wouldn't teach or talk to them about hitting six sixes because six sixes aren't good cricket."

"People always ring me up when anyone repeats the feat," says Nash. "I don't get fed up talking about it. If people want to know, I just tell them as it was – as I best remember. To be honest, I don't get annoyed about always being associated with the six sixes but sometimes it would be really nice if somebody remembered the other things I did in the game.

"I still think Garry was the best cricketer I played against and the best that's ever played the game. People talk about players who bat and bowl and they use the word 'great' far too liberally. Nobody had the ability to do what Garry could do on the cricket field. I don't see it as any disgrace that he hit me for six sixes – just to be on the field with the most gifted cricketer of all time was a privilege. It was just another day in the history of the game. I bowled five reasonably good balls that lesser mortals would not have dealt with in anywhere near the same way. I'm happy to be a part of cricket history. It would have been better if I'd been batting rather than bowling but that's life."

AFTERWORD

W̶riting this book has been a hugely enjoyable and rewarding experience and would not have been possible without the support of a number of people. I am most grateful to Garry Sobers, Malcolm Nash and all the surviving members of the Glamorgan and Nottinghamshire teams for agreeing to share their memories of the six sixes day with me. I would particularly like to thank Malcolm for the considerable amount of time he has spent talking about something which many people in his position would have preferred to forget. I am also grateful to Ravi Shastri and Herschelle Gibbs for discussing their achievements in hitting six sixes in one over in 1985 and 2007.

I would like to thank the following individuals and organisations for their help along the way: Rob Bradley, Lisa Fairclough, Mike Fatkin, Basharat Hassan, Edith Hughes, James Motley, Byron Mugford, Eleanor Pigg, Dave Simmonds, Jodie Thomson, Peter Williams, Martin Williamson, Tony Woolway, the British Newspaper Library, *The Nottingham Evening Post* and the extraordinarily useful CricketArchive website.

A number of the photographs in this book are reproduced by kind permission of their copyright owners and I'm grateful to the following: BBC Wales, Christie's, Wesley David-Scott, Glamorgan County Cricket Club, Huw John, Tom Lloyd, Nottinghamshire County Cricket Club, *Playfair Cricket Monthly*, Pradeep Mandhani, Sky Sports, Peter Walker and Media Wales.

I would particularly like to thank Dr Andrew Hignell, Glamorgan's scorer and archivist, and Peter Wynne-Thomas, Nottinghamshire's archivist and librarian, for supplying me with photographs of the players and information about the match. Andrew, in particular, has been most helpful in providing details of Malcolm Nash's often overlooked career following his famous over in Swansea and the 1968 experimental rule change covering a fair catch.

I would like to express my appreciation to Matthew Engel for his foreword and special thanks must go to my designer, Simon Hicks, who has guided me through the publishing process for the third time; to Peter Walker, one of the Glamorgan fielders on the day, for reading the recollections of his former team-mates with great patience; and to Stephen Chalke, a fellow writer-publisher, who has provided invaluable editorial advice and support from the outset. It goes without saying that any errors are entirely my responsibility.

SCORECARD

Glamorgan v Nottinghamshire
St Helen's, Swansea, 31st August, 1st and 2nd September 1968

Nottinghamshire won the toss and decided to bat

Umpires: JG Langridge, WE Phillipson

Result: Nottinghamshire won by 166 runs

Notts	First Innings		Second Innings	
JB Bolus	c sub (A Rees) b Nash	140	run out	3
RA White	c Wheatley b B Lewis	73	b Cordle	1
G Frost	c AR Lewis b Nash	50	b Nash	2
MJ Smedley	c AR Lewis b Nash	27	c Majid b Cordle	24
+ DL Murray	b Nash	0	c Cordle b Shepherd	13
JM Parkin	not out	15	not out	9
* GS Sobers	not out	76	b Shepherd	72
SR Bielby	did not bat		not out	13
MNS Taylor	did not bat		did not bat	
DJ Halfyard	did not bat		did not bat	
B Stead	did not bat		did not bat	
Extras	(4 b, 7 lb, 2 nb)	13	(1 b, 1 nb)	2
Total	(5 wkts dec, 99 overs)	394	(6 wkts dec, 58 overs)	139

Fall of wickets: 1-126, 2-258, 3-289, 4-289, 5-308   1-2, 2-7, 3-7, 4-30, 5-70, 6-124

Bowling	O	M	R	W	O	M	R	W
Wheatley	5	0	22	0				
Nash	21	3	100	4	17	4	53	1
Cordle	3	1	24	0	16	4	41	2
Walker	32	4	109	0				
Shepherd	25	5	82	0	25	10	43	2
B Lewis	13	1	44	1				

SCORECARD

Glamorgan	First Innings		Second Innings	
A Jones	c Murray b Taylor	25	c Parkin b Taylor	1
RC Davis	c Taylor b Stead	0	b Stead	18
Majid Khan	c Taylor b Halfyard	41	c Bolus b Taylor	4
* AR Lewis	c Bielby b Taylor	0	c Bielby b Whit	52
PM Walker	not out	104	c Sobers b White	16
+ EW Jones	lbw b Sobers	29	c Stead b Taylor	3
EA Cordle	lbw b Halfyard	4	c Smedley b Taylor	4
MA Nash	b Sobers	8	b White	5
B Lewis	run out	38	b Taylor	4
DJ Shepherd	c Sobers b Halfyard	0	b White	4
OS Wheatley	b White	1	not out	0
Extras	(3 lb, 1 w)	4	(2 lb)	2
Total	(all out, 92.2 overs)	254	(all out, 40 overs)	113

Fall of wickets: 1-0, 2-46, 3-56, 4-78, 5-137,
6-142, 7-179, 8-252, 9-253,
10-254

1-40, 2-45, 3-49, 4-85, 5-96,
6-100, 7-100, 8-105, 9-113,
10-113

Bowling	O	M	R	W		O	M	R	W
Sobers	20	6	63	2					
Stead	9	3	27	1		9	1	26	1
Taylor	9	2	23	2		16	6	47	5
Halfyard	31	8	71	3		7	1	29	0
White	23.2	5	66	1		8	5	9	4

In Glamorgan's second innings, Jones and AR Lewis
changed positions because of injury

BIBLIOGRAPHY

Arlott, John, *Alletson's Innings* (Epworth, 1957)

Bailey, Trevor, *Sir Gary: A Biography* (Collins, 1976)

Bearshaw, Brian, *The Big Hitters* (Macdonald Queen Anne Press, 1986)

Blofeld, Henry, *Cricket's Great Entertainers* (Hodder & Stoughton, 2003)

Brodribb, Gerald, *Hit for Six* (Heinemann, 1960)

Foot, David, *Sunshine, Sixes and Cider* (David & Charles, 1996)

Heffer, Simon, *The Daily Telegraph Century of County Cricket: The 100 Best Matches* (Sidgwick & Jackson, 1990)

Hignell, Andrew, *The Skipper – A Biography of Wilf Wooller* (Limlow Books, 1995)

Lemmon, David, *The Wisden Book of Cricket Quotations* (Macdonald Queen Anne Press, 1990)

Lewis, Tony, *Playing Days* (Stanley Paul, 1985)

Lewis, Tony, *Taking Fresh Guard* (Headline, 2003)

Lloyd, Grahame, *Daffodil Days: Glamorgan's Glorious Summer* (Gomer, 1998)

McLellan, Alastair, *The Enemy Within: The Impact of Overseas Players on English Cricket* (Blandford, 1994)

Miller, Douglas, *Born to Bowl: The Life and Times of Don Shepherd* (Fairfield Books, 2004)

Phillips, Barry, *Arthur Wellard: No Mere Slogger* (Leisuresolve, 1996)

Sobers, Garry, *My Autobiography* (Headline, 2002)

Sobers, Sir Garfield, (with Brian Scovell), *Sobers: Twenty Years At The Top* (Macmillan, 1988)

Tibballs, Geoff, *Great Sporting Eccentrics* (Robson Books, 1997)

Walker, Peter, *It's Not Just Cricket* (Fairfield Books, 2006)

Ward, Andrew, *Cricket's Strangest Matches* (Robson Books, 1999)

Wisden Cricketers' Almanack

The Times, The Guardian, The Sunday Express, The Daily Telegraph, The Observer, The People, The Independent, The Independent on Sunday, The South Wales Echo, The Western Mail, The Nottingham Guardian Journal, The Nottingham Evening Post and News, Playfair Cricket Monthly, The Cricketer and *Wisden Cricket Monthly*

The Cricinfo website

The 1968 Glamorgan County Cricket Club Members Newsletter

The 1969 Glamorgan County Cricket Club Yearbook

INDEX

Abberley, Neal 171

Aberavon R.F.C. 74

Aberfan Disaster 176

Afan Lido leisure centre, Port Talbot 183

Ahmed, Saeed 28

Aizazuddin, Faqir 27

Ali, Muhammad 109

Alletson, Ted 9, 17-21, 22, 207

Ames, Bunty 44-5, 150

Ames, Les 26, 44

Amis, Dennis 204

Andrews, Bill 23

Arlott, John 17, 20-1, 101, 113, 174, 175, 181, 202-3

Armanath, Mohinder 159

Armstrong, Tom 22, 24

Arnold, John 78

Arthur, Owen 202

Ashley Down Ground, Bristol 18, 25, 77

Astle, Nathan 25

Aston Villa F.C. 73

Aspinall, Ron 78

Atkin, Ronald 16, 28

Bailey, Trevor 54

Bannister, Roger 13

Barber, Bob 91

Barrington, Ken 86

Basford, near Nottingham 85

Bates, Donald 72

BBC Wales 17, 74, 111, 125, 126, 138, 175, 176, 181, 197

Bedser, Alec 86, 204

Benaud, Richie 103, 110

Bhogle, Harsha 157

Bielby, Richard 54, 191

Billot, John 89

Blofeld, Henry 28, 57

Bolus, Brian 37-8, 39, 48, 50-1, 52, 53, 58, 59, 60, 78, 117-18, 185-6, 189, 192, 193

Booth, Lawrence 33

Botham, Ian 25

Boycott, Geoffrey 37, 176, 200

Brace, Onllwyn 62, 74

Bradman, Don 13, 201-2

Brain, Brian 187

Bramall Lane, Sheffield 122

Breakwell, Dennis 206

Brearley, Mike 204, 205

Brenkley, Stephen 164

British Columbia 177-8, 206

British Lions 74

Broad, Stuart 10, 163-6

Brodribb, Gerald 24

Brown, Tony 43

Burge, Peter 75-6

Buss, Mike 188

California 206, 207

Cambridge University 39, 67, 97, 111, 177

Cardiff Arms Park 21, 75

Cardiff City F.C. 73

Cardus, Neville 32-3, 174

Carlos, John 13

Cartwright, Tom 176

Central Lancashire League 33

Central Recreation Ground, Hastings 22

Chaplin, Bertie 20

Chappell, Greg 68

Cheriton Road Sports Ground, Folkestone 182

Christie's 194, 196

Clarence Park, Weston-super-Mare 73

Claverley Cricket Club, Shropshire 179

Clift, Phil 114

Collingwood, Paul 164

Compton, Denis 34

Connolly, Alan 69

Constantine, Learie 80

Cordle, Tony 49, 52, 67, 80, 91, 101, 123-4, 128, 129, 131-2, 134, 138, 144, 177-9, 180, 196-7

Cordle, Una 177

County Ground, Derby 88, 99, 183

County Ground, Hove 17, 18-21, 67, 71

County Ground, Northampton 44

County Ground, Southampton 87

County Ground, Taunton 41, 88, 92

Cowdrey, Colin 200

Cowgill, Brian 140

Cowper, Bob 69, 88, 115

Cox, George 20

Crabble Athletic Ground, Dover 28, 44

Cricket Board of Wales 176

Cricket Foundation 183

Cricketers, The, Swansea 79, 80, 81

Croft, Robert 157

Cronje, Hansie 159

Davis, Bryan 102, 184

Davis, Roger 27, 79, 87, 96, 99, 100, 102, 106, 109, 111, 112, 113, 121-3, 125-33, 136, 137, 138, 144, 145-6, 147, 170-2, 182, 205

Davies, Haydn 147

de Mille, Cecil B. 16

Dev, Kapil 25, 154

Dewsbury and Savile Ground, 21

Doctrove, Billy 163

D'Oliveira, Basil 13, 169, 180

Dolphin Hotel, The, Swansea 45

Dooland, Bruce 34

Duke & Son of Nottingham cricket balls 195-7

Dyer, Bill 61

East, Ray 125

Eden Gardens, Calcutta 14, 154

Edgbaston, Birmingham 69, 171

INDEX

Edrich, John 37

Edwards, Bill 81, 197

Elm Avenue, Newark 186

Emmett, George 25

Engineer, Farokh 169

England and Wales Cricket Board 175

England Management Advisory Committee (EMAC) 185

ESPN Star Sports 158

Eugene Cross Park, Ebbw Vale 71

Evans, David 114

Flavell, Jack 75

Fletcher, Duncan 172

Flintoff, Andrew 162, 164, 165

Foot, David 22-3

Forbes, Carlton 37, 41, 59

Ford, Trevor 53, 72-3

Foulger, Neville 36, 37

Fountain Inn, The, Pontarddulais 177

Fredericks, Roy 145

Fred's Bar 146

Fred's Shed 146

Frith, David 22

Frost, Graham 35, 41-2, 45-6, 49-51, 52-3, 58, 59, 106, 124, 132-3, 142-3, 186-7, 188-9

Gallagher, Bernard 28

Gandhi, Indira 154

Gavaskar, Sunny 154, 156, 159

Gibbs, Herschelle 10, 159-63, 165

Gibbs, Lance 40

Gibson, Alan 89, 206

Gibson, Pat 90, 105, 194

Gifford, Norman 125, 187

Gilchrist, Adam 25

Gillhouley, Keith 37

Gleeson, John 69, 88

Gloucester Park, Perth 112

Gloucester R.F.C. 174

Gnoll, The, Neath 69

Gough, John 195

Grace, W.G. 13

Grandstand, BBC TV programme 61-3, 140, 150

Graveney, Tom 180

Greig, Tony 188, 204

Griffin, Derek 61

Griffith, Charlie 200

Gunn, George 18, 20

Gunn, John 194

Habitat for Humanity 161

Hadlee, Richard 193

Halfyard, David 40, 43, 88, 143, 192-3

Hall, Wes 37, 204

Hare, Dusty 190

Harries, Alun 146

Harris, Mike 188

Harris, Paul 159

Harvey, Bagenal 34

Harvey, Neil 78

Hassan, Basharat 195

Hawke, Neil 114

Haydock Park 177

Hayes, Frank 205

Haynes, Richard 25

Headingley, Leeds 37, 75-6, 77, 202

Headley, Ron 187

Hignell, Andrew 70, 195

Hill, Gerry 21

Hillary, Edmund 13, 174

Hobbs, Jack 202

Hoey, Brian 149-50

Holford, David 201

Hughes, Pat 144

Hughes, Wilf 22

Hutton, Len 12

Ibadulla, Billy 40-41

Illingworth, Ray 33, 91, 170, 174

International Cavaliers, 31-2, 34

International Cricket Council (ICC) 174, 175, 202, 207

International Teams Management Group 186

Iremonger, James 18

Irvine, Lee 142

Jacklin, Tony 62

Jackman, Robin 205

James, C.L.R. 175

Jayasuriya, Sanath 164

Jenkins, Fred 146

Jessop, Gilbert 155

Jones, Alan 72, 88, 98, 102, 111-14, 115-16, 117, 118, 121, 124, 129, 139, 144, 145, 169-70, 181, 205

Jones, Arthur 18, 19

Jones, Eifion 27, 79, 80, 81, 88, 100, 114-15, 116, 118, 124, 137, 177, 183, 205

Jones, Jeff 67, 70, 71, 72, 180

Joshi, Uday 188

Joslin, Les 88

Kallis, Jacques 160, 161

Kanhai, Rohan 40-41

Kansas 206

Kensington Oval, Bridgetown 45

Khan, Jahangir 97

Khan, Majid 10, 26-8, 68, 79, 80, 81, 88, 91, 96-100, 102, 106-7, 110, 121, 126, 137, 150, 172-4, 184, 207

Killick, Ernest 18, 19, 20

Kimberley, near Nottingham 54, 83, 190

King, Collis 205

King Edward's Road 79, 111, 145

Kitchen, Mervyn 68

Kline, Lindsay 103

Knight, Nick 162

Kookaburra cricket balls 197

Kuala Lumpur, 10

Kumble, Anil 13

Ladbrokes 188

Lake, Emlyn 146

Laker, Jim 13

Langridge, John 129, 130, 131, 141

Lara, Brian 202

Lawry, Bill 77

Leach, George 18, 19, 20

Lee, Garnett 18

Leeds Rugby League Club, 74-5

Lever, John 182-3

Lever, Peter 90

Lewis, Brian 49, 50, 60, 93, 94, 103, 105, 110, 115, 126, 179-80

Lewis, Charles 147-8

Lewis, Colin 171-2

Lewis, Euros 72

Lewis, John (ex-BBC Wales cameraman) 61, 81, 140

Lewis, John 147

Lewis, Richard 147-8, 194, 197

Lewis, Tony 46, 49, 51-2, 53, 57, 58-9, 67, 68, 71, 79, 91, 98, 100, 101, 102, 104, 109-11, 114, 116, 117, 131, 144, 148, 172, 173, 175-6, 180, 181

Lillee, Dennis 201, 202

Llanelli R.F.C. 74

Llewellyn, Mike 205-6

Lloyd, Clive 10, 123, 155

Lockheed Sports Club Ground, Leamington Spa 84

Lord's, London 8, 24-5, 27, 35, 41, 77, 86, 157, 169, 170, 175, 180, 184-5, 201

Luckhurst, Brian 169

Maesteg 86, 180

Maesteg R.F.C. 74

Mallett, Ashley 114

Manselton 146

Manton Colliery, near Worksop 21

Marshall, Eddie 195

Marylebone Cricket Club (MCC) 31, 34, 174, 175, 181

Mascarenhas, Dimitri 25, 163

May, Peter 86

Maynard, Matthew 10, 157

McConnon, Jim 10, 70

Melbourne Cricket Ground 201

Meyer, Barrie 42-3

Miller, Douglas 101

Miller, Josie 195

Milton, Arthur 43

More, Kiran 155-6, 159

Moore, Ian 41

Morgan, Jack 14

Morris, Hugh 157

Moss, Alan 91

Mote Park, Maidstone 76

Mumbles light railway 194

Murray, Deryck 39, 40, 42, 54, 56, 78, 115, 142, 187-8, 189-90

Nanan, Nirmal 190

Nash, Malcolm 8, 9, 48-9, 51-2, 56, 57, 60, 63-4, 66-70, 72, 79, 80, 87, 88, 92-4, 100, 102, 103, 105-7, 109-10, 115, 116, 117, 118-19, 121, 123, 124, 125, 127, 130, 133, 134, 136-51, 171, 175-

6, 177, 179, 180, 188, 191, 196, 196-7, 199, 202-8

Nash, Nhon 207

Nationwide, BBC television programme 176

Neath indoor cricket school 100, 179

Neath R.F.C. 174

New Road, Worcester 192

Newport County 28, 73

Norman, John 61-3, 140

Nottinghamshire Supporters' Association 195

Oates, Tom 18

Old, Chris 204

Old Trafford, Manchester 8, 76

Ormrod, Alan 187

Oval, The, London 51, 76, 101, 157, 163, 164, 180, 181, 205

Packer, Kerry 174

Pakistan Cricket Board 174

Pakistan Television Corporation 174

Palmer, Ken 68

Pardon, Sydney 33-4

Park Road Ground, Loughborough 190

Parkin, Claire 191

Parkin, John 54-5, 56, 59, 60, 63-4, 78, 79, 81, 93-4, 105, 106, 116, 118, 127-8, 137, 141, 142, 169, 189-91

Parkin, Joyce 191

Parkin, Lynne 191

Parkhouse, Gilbert 70, 73

Parkmill, Gower 103, 181

Patil, Sandeep 159

Penllergaer 146

Penrhyn Avenue, Rhos-on-Sea, Colwyn Bay 197

Peters, Martin 16

Philadelphia Cricket Festival 207

Phillips, Barry 24

Phillipson, Eddie 79, 80, 93, 105, 116, 124, 127, 129, 130-2, 136, 137, 141, 143

Phoenix County Ground, Bristol 204

Pontardawe 147-8

Pontarddulais 177

Pontypool R.F.C. 174

Port Talbot, 53, 73, 180

Pressdee, Jim 76-7

Procter, Mike 42, 169

Professional Cricketers' Association 193

PSV Eindhoven F.C. 73

Queen's Park Oval, Port of Spain 199, 202

Radley, Clive 205

Raj, Tilak 155-6

Rajput, Lalchand 154

Rana, Shakoor 183

Randall, Derek 190

Ranji Trophy 153, 156-7

INDEX

Recreational Trust Ground, Lydney 67

Redpath, Ian 69

Rees, Alan 53, 73-9, 80, 81, 93, 183-4

Reid, John 28

Relf, Albert 20

Relf, Robert 20

Rhodes, Wilfred 21

Rice, Clive 193

Richards, Barry 60, 176, 204

Richards, Viv 25, 160, 202

Riley, William 19

Ronaldo, Cristiano 31

Rothmans, tobacco firm 31

Rowden Road, Bath 22, 23-4, 25-6

Royal St George's, Sandwich 62

Sahara Stadium, The, Kingsmead, Durban 164

Severn Estuary 10

Shakespeare, William 150

Shastri, Ravi 10, 13-14, 153-9, 160, 165-6

Shaw, Alfred 194

Sheahan, Paul 91, 115

Shepherd, Don 49, 63, 69, 73, 79, 86-7, 92, 98, 100, 101-5, 106, 111, 113, 115, 117, 130, 138, 140, 173, 174, 181-2, 191

Sherwood, Alf 73

Sidebottom, Ryan 193

Simmons, Jack 193

Sinfield, Reg 25

Singh, Yuvraj 10, 163-6

Skelding, Alec 26

Smart, Cyril 9, 21-2, 207

Smedley, Mike 38-9, 42, 53, 56-7, 59-60, 78, 101, 132, 142, 188-9

Smedley, Shelley 132

Smith, 'Big Jim' 24-5, 207

Smith, Charles 20

Smith, Graeme 159, 160

Smith, Mike 174

Smith, Tommie 13

Snow, John 188

Sobers, Garry 8-9, 10, 13, 14, 16-17, 26, 28-9, 31, 32-46, 54, 55-6, 57-8, 60, 63-4, 66-7, 72, 75, 78, 80, 84, 88, 89, 90, 92-4, 96, 104-7, 109, 111-13, 116, 117-18, 121, 122, 124-5, 127-8, 130, 134, 136-51, 153, 158, 160, 168-9, 170, 174, 177, 179, 182, 183, 184, 185, 186-7, 188, 189, 190-1, 192, 194, 195-6, 197, 199-203, 206-8

Sophia Gardens, Cardiff 70, 71, 76, 88, 98, 173, 180

Spencer, John 188

Sports Council for Wales 183

Staffordshire League 33

Statham, Brian 84, 91

Stead, Barry 193-4

Steele, David 204

Stewart, Mickey 86

St Fagans, near Cardiff 71

St Helen's, Swansea 8, 10, 16, 17, 26, 27-8, 29, 46, 48, 56, 67-8, 69, 71, 76, 77, 78-81, 84, 86, 96,

111, 112, 113, 121-2, 124, 144-7, 157, 162, 168, 171, 177, 183, 184, 193, 194, 196, 197, 205

St Helen's Avenue 79, 111, 139, 196

St Helen's Balconiers 145, 146

St Michael's University School, Victoria 178

Stuart Surridge cricket balls 196-7

Sunderland F.C. 73

Suttle, Ken 188

Swansea Bay 10

Taylor, Derek 206

Taylor, Ken 184

Taylor, Mike 39-40, 43, 191-2, 193

Tenzing Norgay, Sherpa 13, 174

Test Match Special, BBC radio programme 175

This is Your Life, ITV television programme 203

Thomson, Ian 129

Timbuktu 139

Titmus, Freddie 77-8

Todd, Paul 190

Tone, River 23

Tong, Andrew 196

Town Ground, Kettering 69

Town Ground, Worksop 55

Townsend, Peter 28

Trafalgar Road Ground, Southport 43-4

Trent Bridge, Nottingham 8, 18, 31, 33-5, 36, 38-9, 42, 54, 59, 67, 84, 143, 148, 184, 186, 188, 194, 196, 201

Trinidad and Tobago Cricket Board 188

Trueman, Fred 36, 75-6, 91, 122, 204

Turner, Glenn 187

Underwood, Derek 51, 52, 111

United Services Recreation Ground, Portsmouth 22, 45, 60-1

United States Junior Cricket 206-7

University of Victoria, British Columbia 178

Valentine, Bryan 26

Valentine's Park, Ilford 67, 70

van Bunge, Daan 160-3

van Troost, Luuk 162

Vaughan, Michael 162

Venner, Brian 61

Vetch Field, Swansea 28-9

Vine, Joe 21

Vorster, John 13

Vowles, Roger 54

Walcott, Clyde 78

Wales Today, BBC Wales programme 176

Wales Tourist Board 175

Walker, Johnnie, whisky maker 162

Walker, Peter 49, 50, 52, 53, 56, 60, 88, 89, 90-2, 93, 111, 122-4, 130-1, 136-7, 150, 171, 173,

176-7, 196

YouTube 207

Wankhede Stadium, Bombay 154

Ward, Alan 204

Warne, Shane 158, 202

Warner Park, Basseterre, St Kitts 160

Wass, Tom 18, 194

Watkin, Steve 157

Watkins, Allan 70, 123

Weekes, Everton 78, 80

Wellard, Arthur 22-6, 150, 207

Welsh Cricket Association 176

Welsh National Opera 175

Western Australia Cricket Association (WACA) 112

Wheat, Arthur 194-5

Wheatley, Ossie 48-9, 53, 68, 70-2, 74, 79, 81, 104, 110, 111, 124, 132, 133, 144, 173, 182-3, 191

White, Bob 35-6, 40-1, 42-3, 48, 55-6, 59, 90, 118, 132, 143, 184-5, 191

Wilkinson, Phillip 190

Williams, John 145-6

Windows, Tony 42

Wood, Barry 90

Wooller, Wilf 61, 63, 68, 70, 74, 75, 81, 93, 97, 106-7, 116, 118, 125, 126, 127, 130, 133, 138, 139-40, 197

Woolley, Frank 25-6, 150

Worrell, Frank 55, 78

Wright, Charles 77

Wynne-Thomas, Peter 194-5

Also by Grahame Lloyd

Daffodil Days: Glamorgan's Glorious Summer
Jan the Man: From Anfield to Vetch Field (with Jan Molby)
C'mon City! A Hundred Years of the Bluebirds
One Cap Wonders: The Ultimate Claim to Football Fame
One Hell of a Season: Imps, Pilgrims and Tales of the Unexpected
Hard Man, Hard Knocks (with Terry Yorath)